MW00628840

Presented to

———————————————————————————

By

———————————————————————————

Date

———————————————————————————

"A dad's influence is powerful! And nothing is more important than their spiritual influence. That's why I'm glad Mark wrote this book. It's powerful! Dads will want to grow in their wisdom and faith as they read this. And they will! Mark's devotions are short for busy dads and not intimidating for those who have never read much of the Bible. They're clearly written, timely, worth reading, and the practical takeaways are relevant. Dads will be encouraged, not overwhelmed. They'll be confident, not unsure. Because dads will grow, their sons will mature in their faith, too. I'm grateful Mark wrote this book and you will be, too."

Dr. Kathy Koch
Founder, Celebrate Kids, Inc., and the author of *Five to Thrive, 8 Great Smarts*, and other titles

----

"Dads! Whether you have just begun your journey as a dad of boys, or you find yourself a long way down the trail, I commend Trail-Ready: 101 Devotions for Dads with Boys to you. The brief devotions in this book are designed to prompt you to become dads who model strong faith, firm convictions, and courageous actions for your sons. This is not an easy journey! As you apply the lessons in this book to your journey as a dad, may the wisdom found here manifest in irreplaceable quality time with your sons as they start their own journey to become godly and responsible husbands, fathers, and citizens!"

Stuart Michelson
Trail Life USA Board Chairman

"Being a dad is an uphill climb; we can't bring a downhill effort. It's time for fathers to Climb Higher. With Trail-Ready, Mark gives fathers a biblically excellent and practical tool—a guiding light as we climb the mountains before us!"

Dr. Chris Harper
Chief Storyteller & CEO Betterman

"Well done, Mark. Most devotionals make me feel guilty or like I'm being lectured. Instead, Trail-Ready partners with me in my quest to be an authentic Christian and devoted dad. You've given me spiritual insights, practical wisdom, and even daring destinations to share with my sons. Thank you!"

Jay Payleitner
National speaker and best-selling author of *52 Things Sons Need from Their Dads* and *GirlDad*, co-authored with his daughter.

"Mark Hancock is not only a godly husband, an engaged dad, and a skilled leader but he's a good friend. His biblical insights found in these devotions will help men walk worthy and finish strong. Dads need to dive into this content because so much is riding on us discipling our families in Christ! I'm grateful to Mark for putting this together. I'm even more thankful to him for modeling the way and helping me on my own journey."

Kent Evans
Author and Co-Founder of Manhood Journey

TRAIL-READY:

101

DEVOTIONS
FOR DADS WITH BOYS

**WORTHY
TRAILMAN**
PRESS

Book Design: Anna Jelstrom
Cover Design: Greg Lane

While the author has made every effort to provide accurate telephone numbers and internet addresses at the time of publication, neither the publisher nor the author assumes any responsibility for errors or for changes that occur after publication.

ISBN 978-1-7330259-6-6

First Edition.

Printed in the United States of America.

Acknowledgements

Projects like this are a collaborative effort of so many, including the writers of the *Raising Godly Boys Minute* podcast and radio broadcast.

Special thanks to those directly responsible for organizing and locating the multitude of photos, trail research, and more. I can't possibly name everyone who had a part, but special thanks to our 2023 Summer Interns Jake Dodson, Levi Durkee, Taylor Hancock, and Joshua Tarver, and staffers Margaret Olson and Matthew Gidney.

Contents

Foreword

Ready to Hit the Trail?

From Mark T. Hancock, CEO of Trail Life USA

Hey, Dad. If you've got a son, then he probably loves gadgets and gizmos. But even the coolest toys and tech don't compare to the time you'll share with him.

That's because life isn't about the abundance of things. It's about love and relationships. And those relationships take time and trust.

Introducing *Trail-Ready: 101 Devotions for Dads with Boys*. Each devotion contains:

- Bible verses — to help you dig into God's Word
- Devotional thoughts — to teach and encourage
- Discussion questions — to prompt practical application
- Reflective photos — beautiful images of day hikes for you to ponder or pursue.

The dad-journey isn't always easy, but moments of connecting make the trail a little less bumpy. And with tips, insights, and guidance from this devotional, you can create meaningful memories that will last a lifetime.

‹ **CALIFORNIA** › The Lady Bird Johnson Grove Trail, near Orick, California, is a 1.5-miles loop in **Redwood National Park**. This low-difficulty trail showcases the stunning redwoods of northern California and can easily connect you with some of the national park's other trails. Take it slow and soak up the lush redwood forest surroundings. 🥾

Rooted

". . . as you received Christ Jesus the Lord, so walk in him, rooted and built up in him and established in the faith."
— Colossians 2:6-7

The world's tallest tree towers 380 feet above the ground in California's Redwood National Park. Named Hyperion, this tree (which is taller than the Statue of Liberty) began as a tiny seed, no bigger than a grain of rice.

Growing into a giant tree didn't happen overnight. Little by little, day by day, the tree dug its roots deep into the soil to establish a solid foundation. This foundation enabled it to grow tall and strong.

Boys can also grow tall and strong, but it takes time and patience. As a father, you play a crucial role in helping your son grow to his full potential.

Your son looks up to you. He hears your words and sees your facial expressions. Before long, he begins imitating your actions. By showing your son how to establish a strong foundation in God's Word, he can develop strong character that will help him succeed throughout life.

CLIMB	Your son is watching you. What kind of example are you setting?
HIGHER	When the storm clouds of life roll in, are you firmly rooted to the rock of your salvation?

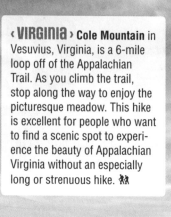

‹ **VIRGINIA** › **Cole Mountain** in Vesuvius, Virginia, is a 6-mile loop off of the Appalachian Trail. As you climb the trail, stop along the way to enjoy the picturesque meadow. This hike is excellent for people who want to find a scenic spot to experience the beauty of Appalachian Virginia without an especially long or strenuous hike. 🚶🚶

Hours and Minutes

"So teach us to number our days that we may get a heart of wisdom."
— Psalm 90:12

02

Boys love statistics—the craziest the better! For instance, did you know that the average American eats around 23 pounds of ice cream a year? Talk about brain freeze!

Here's another statistic: Each year contains 8,760 hours (or 525,600 minutes). That's a huge number. But how are you spending your time throughout the year?

- How long did you stare at your phone yesterday?
- How many hours did you watch TV this week?
- How many minutes did you spend time with or pray for your son this month?

The days, weeks, and months are quickly passing. Don't let insignificant things distract you from time with your family. Be intentional in how you invest your time in your son's life.

Here's a simple idea to get you started. Hop in the car and visit a nearby ice cream shop. As you share that dedicated one-on-one space, you'll create memories that will last a lifetime. You'll also be at your 23 pounds of ice cream in no time!

CLIMB	When you're 75 years old, what current activities will you recognize as a waste of time?
HIGHER	What activities will you wish you had spent more time on?

‹ NEW YORK › **Taughannock Falls State Park**, located near Trumansburg, New York, is best known for its majestic 215-foot waterfall. Resting against the banks of Cayuga Lake, Taughannock Falls can be accessed via the North Rim and Gorge Trail, a 3.5-mile out-and-back hike. 🚶🚶

Tug of War

"For we do not wrestle against flesh and blood, but against the rulers, against the authorities, against the cosmic powers over this present darkness, against the spiritual forces of evil in the heavenly places." — **Ephesians 6:12**

Did you ever play tug of war as a kid? Do you remember pulling and heaving on a thick rope, trying to yank the other team in your direction?

A game of tug of war continues to this day. But instead of two teams pulling on a rope, today's anti-Christian culture is pulling your son away from traditional, biblical values.

One of these values is the time-tested realization that boys and girls are different. In this societal tug of war, misguided activists insist that boys and girls are completely the same.

But they aren't.

In addition to physical differences, boys and girls have mental and emotional differences. And that's okay. In fact, that's normal and healthy.

Don't let confusing ideology pull your son in the wrong direction. There is a path ahead, but it requires you to help guide your son in the way he should go.

CLIMB HIGHER

If you have several kids, do you compare their physical, mental, and spiritual growth? Is this fair?

Think of one way you can encourage your kids today.

‹ **COLORADO** › The Palmer, Cabin Canyon, and Central Gardens loop in the **Garden of the Gods** is an easy day hike featuring beautiful rock formations in one of the best-known natural landmarks in Colorado. You'll gain 593 feet in elevation along this 4-mile loop trail, a nice reward for a highly accessible hike within the Colorado Springs city limits. 🥾

Playdough

"The LORD will fulfill his purpose for me; your steadfast love, O LORD, endures forever. Do not forsake the work of your hands." — Psalm 138:8

Boys love playdough. They squeeze it and stretch it. They roll it into skinny snakes and smoosh it into clumps.

As dads, we can sometimes feel like playdough. We get squeezed for time and attention. Then we get stretched this way and that way. We feel squashed by the demands of life.

When the routines of being a dad feel overwhelming, realize that you're not alone. Instead of growing frustrated at life, take a moment to adjust your perspective. Realize that you're a work in progress.

Because you are in God's hands, He is shaping you into His likeness, forming your character into a useful masterpiece.

Boys make wild and wacky objects with playdough, but in the master Sculptor's hands, your fathering efforts are being transformed into something beautiful. So, don't give up. That squeezing and stretching is just part of the process.

CLIMB HIGHER

Do you feel pulled and stretched by your fathering responsibilities? If so, remember that you're simply called to faithful service. The results are in the Lord's hands.

‹ **CONNECTICUT** › The Toby's Rock Mountain Outer Loop is a 2.7-mile hike through Connecticut's **Naugatuck State Forest**, near the quiet town of Beacon Falls. As you follow the rocky path through the valley, you'll encounter multiple waterfalls and clearings with great views of the surrounding hills. 🚶🚶

Juggling

"Let each of you look not only to his own interests, but also to the interests of others." — **Philippians 2:4**

05

I f you've ever been to a circus, you've seen clowns juggling balls and clubs. Juggling may seem simple enough, but it's actually a lot harder than it looks.

Parenting boys can also be harder than you expect. You're trying to juggle schedules, manage conflicts, and adapt to various personalities. And many times, you hardly have enough time to deal with one issue before another one comes flying at you.

Fortunately, you don't have to be a clown to successfully juggle the requirements of being a dad. Simply begin with love, toss in patience, and throw in a bunch of fun.

As you practice, there will be times that you drop the ball. Other times, you'll get confused with so many moving parts. But by staying focused on your family, you'll see that juggling parenthood isn't actually so difficult. And before you know it, both you and your son will be smiling from ear to ear.

CLIMB HIGHER

The more responsibilities you try to juggle, the harder it becomes. Is there a way to simplify your life so that you can devote extra time to your son?

‹ UTAH › Delicate Arch Trail in **Arches National Park**, near Moab, Utah, is a 3.2-mile out-and-back journey famous for its legendary rock formation. Whatever you do, don't miss the striking geological features along the way. Delicate Arch Trail is one of the most popular trails in the park, the arch providing an intriguing subject for photographers. 🥾

Failure Isn't Final

*". . . The Lord is faithful in all his words
and kind in all his works.
The Lord upholds all who are falling and
raises up all who are bowed down."*
— **Psalm 145:13-14**

One of the greatest inventions of the 19th century was the lightbulb. But creating the light bulb required lots of trial and error. A reporter once asked Thomas Edison, "How did it feel to fail 1,000 times?" Edison replied, "I didn't fail 1,000 times. The light bulb was an invention with 1,000 steps."

Edison was right. Achievement takes time and a whole lot of determination. That's because failure is a part of life. In fact, it's normal and natural. And even though no one likes to fail, it teaches us to do better and to strive harder as we reach for our goals.

Boys need to be challenged in life. It's a way of helping them grow and test their limits. But even though trying something new may result in failure, that failure helps them develop important character traits that are essential for future success.

Don't shield your son from the possibility of failure. When you do that, you are quietly telling him you don't believe he's capable.

CLIMB HIGHER

Are you helping your son learn from failure? Are you helping him stretch his potential through age-appropriate challenges?

When your son doesn't see immediate success, how do you respond? Do you grow frustrated, or do you continue to provide encouraging support?

‹ **WEST VIRGINIA** › Located in **Coopers Rock State Park** near Morgantown, West Virginia, Rattlesnake Trail is a 4.1-mile loop accessible via the Rhododendron to Ridge trails. The Rattlesnake portion of the trail is particularly challenging, requiring hikers to scramble up the rugged rocks through which the trail weaves. Soak up the great views and check out the curious caves and rock formations along the way. 🥾

Tools of the Trade

"Fathers, do not provoke your children to anger, but bring them up in the discipline and instruction of the Lord."
— Ephesians 6:4

07

D id you ever try to cut a 2x4 with a hacksaw? Hammering a nail with a wrench is just as difficult. That's why having the right tool makes all the difference in successfully completing a job.

When it comes to training boys, using the right tools also makes a big difference. God's Word is our go-to resource. From it, we learn important truths and principles that guide us in training our sons.

Ephesians 6:4 says that discipline is necessary in helping our sons grow into godly men. But discipline must be balanced by love and attention. If you want your son to listen to correction, make sure you provide encouragement as well.

Discipline. Love. Attention. Encouragement. All great tools for correction. All with specific functions.

The parenting toolbox contains many other important tools, too. The more you understand the purpose of each, the more likely you'll use them at the right time and for the right job.

CLIMB HIGHER

When correction is necessary, is it fair and balanced? Have you considered different techniques that might be more effective?

‹ **Texas** › Located in the Chisos Mountain Basin, Lost Mine Trail in **Big Bend National Park** provides incredible views for miles in all directions. Showcasing the rugged beauty of the Chihuahuan Desert of southwest Texas, the 5-mile trail features juniper, oak, and pine clusters. Sierra del Carmen and Pine Canyon are visible at the summit, and Casa Grande provides an excellent backdrop for photos. 🚶🚶

Competition

"In all these things we are more than conquerors through him who loved us."
— **Romans 8:37**

08

Boys love to wrestle. They embrace the challenge and excitement competition brings. As they compete, they experience the thrill of victory and, sometimes, the agony of defeat.

Boys desperately need this. Too often the only thing they wrestle with is boredom. They sit on the couch and stare at their phones. This isn't physically, mentally, or spiritually healthy.

Don't forget that boys grow by being challenged. Through persistence, failure, recovery, success, and determination, they learn to conquer obstacles. As a dad, encourage your son to compete. This often involves sports, but it could also include music, art, academic clubs, and other hobbies and outdoor activities.

When you shield your son from opportunities where you are afraid he may not win, you are subtly telling him you don't think he is capable. But when your son realizes that he can accomplish hard things, he'll develop important character traits that will help him succeed throughout life.

CLIMB	As a dad, are you encouraging your son to try new activities?
HIGHER	When he competes and doesn't immediately win, what advice do you give him?

‹ **WASHINGTON** › Located in **Mount Baker Snoqualmie National Forest** near Skykomish, Washington, the Deception Falls Interpretive Trail leads hikers along a 0.6-mile loop following Deception Creek to where it meets the Tyee River. The route offers hikers a chance to soak up the splendor of Deception Creek Falls. The multi-tiered waterfall and vibrant evergreens make this a memorable day hike for those looking for a quick venture into the beautiful northern Washington wilderness. 🚶🚶

Held Captive

"See to it that no one takes you captive by philosophy and empty deceit, according to human tradition, . . ."
— **Colossians 2:8**

A battle rages, and boys are on the front lines. They're in danger of being captured by anti-Christian philosophies like:

- Relativism—which says that there are no absolutes in life. It argues that truth, knowledge, and even morality is whatever a person wants it to be.
- Humanism—which teaches that a person must depend on himself to reach his full potential. If this is true, then why do we even need God?
- Materialism—which is the accumulation of stuff. Luke 12:15 says, "Take care, and be on your guard against all covetousness, for one's life does not consist in the abundance of his possessions."

Training your son in today's secular culture isn't easy. It requires time and attention. Don't let worldly philosophies capture your son, destroying his faith in Christ. Teach him to build his foundation on the solid Word of God.

CLIMB HIGHER

The world is battling to control your son's mind. How are you helping him discern what is right from wrong?

When you see evil in the world, do you point it out, or do you hide from it?

‹ **Montana** › An easy drive from Bozeman, Montana, **Custer Gallatin National Forest** is a natural wonderland, with sparkling blue lakes, majestic mountain peaks, enchanting meadows, and beautiful evergreens. The Ross Peak trail is a strenuous 8.4-mile hike with 1,755 feet of elevation gain, making this a great day-hike for more experienced hikers. 🥾

Winter Gear

"Be watchful, stand firm in the faith, act like men, be strong."— **1 Corinthians 16:13**

If you live in the north, winter winds blow in snow, ice, and freezing temperatures. Before sending your boys outside to go sledding, you wrap them in coats, hats, and gloves. This clothing keeps them protected from the harsh elements outside the home.

Your boys experience other harsh elements outside the home. They're called peer pressure, bullying, and temptation. Without knowledge of how to withstand these destructive forces, boys are quickly overwhelmed.

Equip your boys to face the world. Have a heart-to-heart talk with your son about important topics or situations he may face at school or on the playground. A good way to 'break the ice' is to tell your son a story about when you were a kid. What lessons did you learn? What do you wish you had known back then?

The more time you spend with your son, the more likely he'll listen to your advice. This will provide him the gear to journey through life with confidence.

CLIMB HIGHER

How are you equipping your son to face the world?

What Bible verses would encourage him to stand strong, even when the world is cold and cruel to Christians?

‹ **WISCONSIN** › The Sentinel Ridge Trail, which overlooks the Mississippi River, cuts through **Wyalusing State Park** near Bagley, Wisconsin. This 3.3-mile out-and-back route features steep climbs with rewarding views. Benches near some of the overlooks allow hikers to sit and marvel at the mighty Mississippi River. 🥾🥾

Love, Spelled T-I-M-E

"Encourage one another and build one another up, just as you are doing."
— **1 Thessalonians 5:11**

Around 7,000 languages are spoken throughout the world. But to communicate with your son, you don't have to be a linguistic expert. In fact, you don't even have to be bilingual. All you need is a desire to spend quality time with him.

This language of love is best demonstrated through action. Play catch with your son. Go fishing together. Visit a national park and explore God's creation.

By spending time with your son, you speak to both his heart and mind. In this way, you show him through action that you love him. And when he knows that you genuinely care for him, he'll be more likely to listen when you provide correction and instruction.

By taking time to communicate with your son in both word and deed, you prepare the way for him to grow into a godly young man.

CLIMB HIGHER

When was the last time you told your son that you love him? Even though it may not seem like a big deal, those words make a huge impression.

Another excellent use of language is through encouragement. Compliment your son within the next 24 hours. As soon as you do, you'll see his face light up with a smile.

‹ **DELAWARE** › **White Clay State Park** stretches from the campus of Princeton University in Newark, Delaware, up to Landenburg, Pennsylvania. The Yeatman Station Road Loop which begins north of Thompson, Delaware, is a 5.9-mile trek. In the spring, the forest surrounding White Clay Creek is speckled with wildflowers, making this a great trail to explore as the winter frost begins to thaw. 🚶‍♂️

Behind Bars

"Behold, children are a heritage from the Lord." — Psalm 127:3

Prison is a hard place. It's cold and cruel, and those locked behind iron bars face loneliness, depression, and bitterness. But the pain of prison extends beyond concrete walls and barbed wire fences.

According to Prison Fellowship, over 1.5 million kids have an incarcerated parent. Of this number, around 92% are fathers. That's around 1.38 million dads in prison. What a sad statistic!

This means that hundreds of thousands of boys are growing up without a dad. And without a proper role model to teach, encourage, and love them, boys are increasingly angry and destructive.

Break the cycle. Be active in your son's life. Recognize the privilege you have of being a father. Show your son that God's Word provides guidance about how to navigate the pathway of life. Show him that you care and that you're committed to helping him grow into a godly young man.

Another way to make a difference is by being "dad-like" to a boy who doesn't have a dad.

CLIMB HIGHER

Even if you aren't incarcerated, are you imprisoned by other activities?

Do you spend more time with your phone than with your family? Did you talk with your son at the dinner table last night?

‹ **Maine** › **Baxter State Park**, situated at the base of Mt. Katahdin, provides hikers with a chance to immerse themselves in the rugged and remote beauty of northern Maine. The Chimney Pond Trail is a 6.3-mile trek with views of stunning glacial ponds and imposing peaks. The trail itself, however, is mostly flat, winding in and out of evergreen woods. 🚶

The Value of Work

13

"Whatever you do, work heartily, as for the Lord and not for men."
— **Colossians 3:23**

After a long day at work, you park your car in the driveway and step out of the vehicle. But before you even reach the front door, your son darts out to greet you.

"Hey, Dad. My friend just got a brand-new drone. It's the SkyMaster 2200. Can I have one too?"

How do you respond?

We all know that boys like toys. Frisbees and basketballs are inexpensive. But other toys, like electric scooters or remote-controlled drones, can cost a lot.

While toys can help kids grow physically and mentally, there's value in having your son work for the things he wants.

Younger kids can complete extra chores. Teenage boys should be given even greater responsibility. That might mean mowing lawns, washing cars, or getting a part-time job.

As you help your son understand the value of hard work and how it relates to money, you're preparing him to succeed in life. And that's a job well done.

CLIMB

HIGHER

When you were a kid, did you ever work extra chores to pay for a special gadget? How did that affect how you took care of it?

What stories from your own life could you tell your son about the importance of taking care of possessions?

‹ **MARYLAND** › The **Blockhouse Point Park** Loop, located near North Potomac, Maryland, is a 7-mile hike along the Potomac River. The trail cuts through a densely forested landscape with some mild climbs in elevation. From various vista points, you'll enjoy excellent views of the historic Potomac landscape. 🚶‍♂️

Escape the Hamster Wheel

14

"The thief comes only to steal and kill and destroy. I came that they may have life and have it abundantly." — **John 10:10**

If you had a pet hamster as a kid, you know those fuzzy furballs love running. Give them a hamster wheel, and they'll run on it day after day.

Similarly, the routines of life can sometimes make us feel as if we're running on a hamster wheel.

While there's certainly value in developing life routines, it's important for boys to experience times of adventure beyond the norms of life. Their minds and bodies crave action and excitement. They need physical and mental challenges that motivate them to work hard. This, in turn, helps them grow into responsible men.

One of the best places to help boys grow and have fun is in the great outdoors. Take your son on a hike. Paddle a canoe. Take him four-wheeling.

Every once in a while, it's important to leave the hamster wheel behind. The thrill of adventure will not be forgotten—by you or your son.

CLIMB HIGHER

Do you feel stuck on a hamster wheel? If so, think of at least one fun activity you and your son could enjoy this month. Next, begin planning that outing. Then be prepared for lots of laughs and memories when you take your son on that adventure.

‹ **KENTUCKY** › Containing some of the more unique geological features in the southeastern United States, Kentucky's **Red River Gorge Geological Area** features breathtaking views and spectacular rock formations. The Rock Bridge Trail is a 1.4-mile loop highlighted by views of a waterfall and a natural stone arch. 🚶🚶

Google Isn't the Answer

"My son, be attentive to my words; incline your ear to my sayings. Let them not escape from your sight; keep them within your heart." — **Proverbs 4:20-21**

When you need information, whom do you ask? If you're like most people, you ask Siri, Alexa, ChatGPT, or Google.

These days, Google is so popular that it processes over 8 billion questions and searches each day! That's fine when it comes to knowing what temperature to bake a ham, or how to install a doorknob. But when it comes to raising your son, don't let the internet take charge.

Boys need to be guided through life—and fathers play a vital role in this process. Begin by helping your son develop a solid foundation in God's Word. When he understands how God wants him to live, he will be able to distinguish right from wrong. This, in turn, will help him avoid disastrous consequences.

YouTube, Twitter, and Instagram aren't the places for boys to learn character, purpose, and leadership. Instead, you have the responsibility (and privilege) of guiding your son as he grows into a young man.

And that's a fact you don't need to Google.

CLIMB HIGHER

Who is guiding your son through life?

When was the last time you talked to your son about age-appropriate challenges he is facing? How can you connect with him more effectively in the future?

‹ SOUTH DAKOTA ›

Devil's Bathtub in **Black Hills National Forest**, South Dakota, is a 1.6-mile out-and-back trail. Because this route is a moderately difficult yet technical hike, come prepared for multiple water crossings and slippery rocks. This trail is an excellent way to explore the rugged Spearfish Canyon, lined with stark rock formations as well as a waterfall and pool at the end of the trail. 🚶🚶

Marriage Is Under Attack

"Husbands, love your wives, as Christ loved the church and gave himself up for her." — **Ephesians 5:25**

The U.S. Census Bureau reports that around 30% of American kids live in homes where either the mother or father is absent. That's an incredibly sad statistic.

More often than not, the father is the one missing from the home. This leaves boys without a role model and without a father's guidance and correction.

The result? Many boys suffer greater behavioral, emotional, and social problems than boys with a father in the home. Because of this, they may seek love in unhealthy and unwholesome places.

The more your son–or a boy without a dad– sees how a man of character acts, talks, and serves, the more he'll want those same biblical values in his own life.

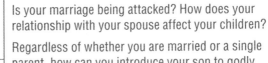

CLIMB HIGHER

Is your marriage being attacked? How does your relationship with your spouse affect your children?

Regardless of whether you are married or a single parent, how can you introduce your son to godly mentors who reinforce the instruction you provide at home? (Hint: check out the excellent programs offered by Trail Life USA.)

‹ **Montana** › Saint Mary and Virginia Falls Trail is a popular attraction in **Glacier National Park**, Montana. The trail runs parallel to Virginia Creek and passes by several waterfalls and beautiful lakes along the way. At 3.1 miles, this trail is one of the easier ones in the park. Although short, it is well worth exploring to see water gushing down majestic mountains. 🚶🚶

Sink or Swim

17

"No temptation has overtaken you that is not common to man. God is faithful, and he will not let you be tempted beyond your ability." — **1 Corinthians 10:13**

When your son was two or three years old, he probably clung tightly to you in the swimming pool. To him, the water looked incredibly deep and scary. But as he learned to splash around, he eventually gained confidence to swim and have fun.

As he continues to grow, don't let him flounder and sink in life. Is peer pressure pulling him down into confusion? Is temptation drowning him in sin?

Teach your son how to avoid these weights by pursuing friendships and activities that are true, honest, and pure. This doesn't come naturally, but through intentional thought, prayer, and action he will remain buoyant through the uplifting of God's strength.

Your son needs to be guided and inspired. Help him swim the distance through consistent training—one lap at a time.

CLIMB HIGHER

What areas of life appear scary for your son? Does he feel comfortable talking to you about challenges he is facing?

Talking about temptation can be awkward and uncomfortable. Despite that, show leadership by talking with your son about his heart and mind. Study the life of Joseph with your son for extra clues on how to live a life that honors the Lord. (Genesis 37-50)

‹ **WYOMING** › With an amazing view of the Teton mountain range in the background, the Schwabacher's Landing Trail is popular among hikers, runners, and birdwatchers in **Grand Teton National Park**. This 0.5-mile out-and-back trail runs alongside the Snake River and provides incredible views for a relatively easy-going hike near Moose, Wyoming. 🚶

Choose Peace over Fear

18

"Fear not, for I am with you; be not dismayed, for I am your God; I will strengthen you, I will help you, I will uphold you with my righteous right hand."
— Isaiah 41:10

Today's world is a dangerous place.
- Hurricanes destroy homes.
- School shootings shatter childhood safety.
- Angry mobs loot stores and set buildings on fire.

And then there are terrorists, drugs, and racial tensions. Add to that health issues and financial problems. The list of worries and fears goes on and on.

Yet the Lord tells us that despite the chaos surrounding us, we can have peace. In John 14:27, the Lord says, "Peace I leave with you; my peace I give to you. Not as the world gives do I give to you. Let not your hearts be troubled, neither let them be afraid."

As you guide your son through life, be intentional in choosing peace over fear. By reminding him that the Lord reigns supreme, you can show him how to be joyful and confident—even through the turmoil of life.

CLIMB HIGHER

TV and social media highlight the worst of human behavior. Because of that, it's easy to see the destruction around us and become fearful of the future. In whom are you placing your hope and confidence?

How does your son respond to fear? What verses could help him remember that God is in control?

‹ **Nevada** › **Cathedral Gorge State Park**, near Panaca, Nevada, is popular for its stark desert landscape adorned with photogenic, jagged rock formations. The Hawk's Ridge Trail is a 4.2-mile loop that leads hikers along a ridge with views of the high desert scenery and the valley below. Sagebrush and desert wildflowers can be seen along the trail, depending on the time of year and recent rainfall.

Hiking in the Dark

"The steps of a man are established by the Lord, when he delights in his way."
— **Psalm 37:23**

19

When hikers are out in the woods, it's easy for everything to look the same, especially when darkness descends. That's why skilled hikers rely on a compass that points due north. By relying on the compass to help them navigate through uncertain terrain, hikers arrive at their destination without the hassle and headache of getting lost.

Boys of all ages need direction in today's dark culture. The world shouts at them from all directions, trying to lure them away from the path of righteousness. Because of this, it's easy for boys to grow confused and frustrated as secular philosophies lead them into treacherous territory.

Help your son understand that God's Word is a compass that will guide him through the hills and valleys of life. Worldly ways have distracted many travelers. But by relying on the truths of the Bible, your son will confidently hike forward in the right direction.

CLIMB	How important is the Bible to you? Does your son see you studying its pages and applying its truths to your daily life?
HIGHER	Are other people pointing your son in the right direction? Are his friends a good influence, or are they making him veer off course?

‹ **GEORGIA** › The Providence Canyon Perimeter Loop is a 2.1-mile hike in **Providence Canyon State Park**. Located near Omaha, Georgia, this "Little Grand Canyon" is a beautiful place for hiking, running, and birding. This scenic trail is a gorgeous place to visit any time of the year, but especially in the fall. 🥾

Shining for Jesus

"And those who are wise shall shine like the brightness of the sky above; and those who turn many to righteousness, like the stars forever and ever." — **Daniel 12:3**

If you step outside tonight and gaze into the night sky, you might notice Sirius—the brightest star visible from earth. Even though it's located over 50 trillion miles away, it still shines brightly in the darkness of space. That's because it's actually more than 25 times brighter than our own sun!

Your son can also shine brightly in today's dark world. Teach him to honor the Lord by doing what is right. This involves helping him understand that swearing, talking disrespectfully about teachers, and laughing at crude jokes is wrong.

Of course, shining for Jesus isn't easy. But by training your son to love God and obey His Word, he can stand against the darkness and point his friends to the ultimate Light of the world. And, as always, being a witness for the Lord Jesus is a really bright idea.

CLIMB HIGHER

Does your son see you shining as a light in today's dark world? Do your words and actions point people to Jesus?

Think of an activity you and your son could do together that would help people know more about God. What's one specific way you could shine as a light to your family as well as to those within your community?

‹ **Hawaii** › Makapu'u Point Lighthouse Trail in Waimanalo, Hawaii, is a 2-mile hike. Located within **Kaiwi State Scenic Shoreline**, this trail offers breathtaking views of Oahu's coast. The trail provides wildlife viewing opportunities, including various Hawaiian seabirds. In November through May, hikers may also see migrating humpback whales along the coast. 🥾

Keep on Keeping On

"He gives power to the faint, and to him who has no might he increases strength."
— Isaiah 40:29

21

Boys love to run. They seem to be constantly dashing, darting, and scurrying around. And when they get older, they run even faster . . . which makes keeping up with them even more work.

Parenting is exhausting. In addition to school and church, there are sports practices, music lessons, and a whole bunch of other activities that take time and energy. Maybe you wish you could just shut everything down to rest for a few days (or weeks)!

In the busyness of everyday life, it's natural to feel tired and overwhelmed. It's important, however, not to let these emotions discourage you. Instead, take heart.

1 Chronicles 16:11 says, "Seek the Lord and his strength; seek his presence continually!" What a great reminder that our help comes from the Lord.

So even though the parenting journey may seem long—keep on keeping on! Your efforts are making a difference—probably more than you'll ever know.

CLIMB

HIGHER

Parenting is emotionally draining. Are you taking time to refresh yourself? How specifically are you doing that?

When life feels overwhelming, are there activities you could delegate to others? Or are there certain activities that are no longer necessary?

‹ **MISSOURI** › Tucked away in **Mark Twain National Forest**, not far from Alton, Missouri, is Greer Springs Trail, a great fit for hikers looking for some peace and quiet. This 1.4-mile hike wanders through old-growth forests en route to the lively Greer Springs. 🚶🚶

Ups and Downs

"Let us then with confidence draw near to the throne of grace, that we may receive mercy and find grace to help in time of need." — **Hebrews 4:16**

22

As a kid, did you ever jump on a trampoline? If so, you probably tried seeing how high you could leap. Yet every time you soared upward, you eventually came back down.

As a dad, you understand that your son's journey through childhood also involves "highs" and "lows." Maybe he earns a perfect grade on a math test. Or perhaps he scores a goal on the soccer field. You cheer from the sidelines, whooping and hollering with excitement.

The "highs" of childhood are great, but "lows" are also a good opportunity for growth. When your son misses an easy layup on the basketball court, or he forgets the notes during a music competition, your reaction will influence whether he grows discouraged or determined.

Life isn't perfect. We know that. But by encouraging your son to bounce back from the "lows" of life, you teach him how to strive forward to reach his full potential.

CLIMB HIGHER

How do you react when life grows hard? Do you become grumpy and impatient? Do you ignore your family?

When your son experiences frustration, how do you respond? What's something you could specifically do or say that would help him rebound from a "low"?

‹ **WYOMING** › The Upper Geyser Basin Trail is a gorgeous hike in Wyoming's legendary **Yellowstone National Park**. This 3.5-mile loop will introduce hikers to one of the park's most popular attractions: geysers. Soak in the pristine scenery along the hike and don't forget to look out for bears and bison. 🚶🚶

The Donut Hole

*"I have no greater joy than to hear that
my children are walking in the truth."*
— 3 John 1:4

23

The average American eats 31 donuts a year. Some eat fewer, but boys probably eat more than their fair share.

Talking about donuts, have you ever wondered why there's a hole in the middle? Because donuts are fried in oil, the hole allows the dough to cook evenly, without the outside becoming burnt and the inside remaining doughy.

In addition to being a tasty treat, the donut is a good reminder. Don't leave a hole in your son's training. Education is certainly important, but don't leave a hole in his social, emotional, and spiritual development.

Here's an idea: take your son to a local donut shop to share some of that donut goodness. While there, have a heart-to-heart talk with your son. Listen as he talks about what's going on at school. Then share some advice—and pray for him.

"Dough-nut" let your son be ill-prepared for life's journey. Train him in the way he should go.

CLIMB HIGHER

When you talk with your son, is your conversation one sided? Do you do all the talking, or do you carefully listen to him?

Are you helping your son reach his full potential? We often pay close attention to his physical and educational development, but are you doing enough to help him grow spiritually?

‹ VERMONT › Located in some of the most remote country on the east coast, Vermont's **Smugglers Notch State Park** offers a variety of excellent day hikes. One of the most picturesque is the 2.1-mile Sterling Pond Trail which leads hikers to Sterling pond. Even though the trail is rocky with nearly 1,000 feet of elevation gain, the views from the pond are mesmerizingly tranquil. 🚶‍♂️

Fear Not

*"I sought the Lord, and he answered me
and delivered me from all my fears."*
— **Psalm 34:4**

24

Are you easily scared?

The command to not be afraid is repeated throughout the Bible. Not just occasionally, but hundreds of times! This repetition seems overblown, but God knew we needed the reminder.

This is especially true when we consider the many secular influences that are trying to conquer the hearts and minds of our sons. The war on gender, the ridicule of biblical teaching, the erosion of traditional values—these and many other "monsters" threaten to scare Christians into inaction and unbelief.

When the sinful ugliness of today's world attacks your son, teach him to stand strong on the solid Word of God. One of the best ways to do this is by memorizing Scripture. When fears attack him, the sword of the Spirit will vanquish foes. Is he using God's Word to move confidently into the future?

**CLIMB
HIGHER**

How important is Scripture memorization to you? If it's been a while since you or your son have memorized a Bible verse, take up the challenge. Learn a Bible verse together. Once you've both committed that Bible passage to heart, reward your effort with a fun and fantastic activity. In this way, you'll help your son to not only survive the "monsters" of life, but also thrive as he grows into a godly young man.

‹ NEBRASKA › Chimney Rock, the crown jewel of the **Chimney Rock National Historic Park** near Scottsbluff, Nebraska, is a striking rock formation that would look right at home in the rugged high deserts of Utah or Arizona. The 1.5-mile out-and-back hike to the rock is also a historically significant excursion as it marks a famous landmark along the legendary Oregon Trail. 𝕏

I'm Bored

"For while bodily training is of some value, godliness is of value in every way, as it holds promise for the present life and also for the life to come." — **1 Timothy 4:8**

Have you ever heard your son say, "I'm bored"? If so, you're not alone.

Part of the reason boys feel bored is because they aren't physically active. TV, video games, and social media are part of the problem. They trap boys in make-believe worlds that soak the fun out of real life.

According to the American Academy of Child & Adolescent Psychiatry, kids spend an average of four to six hours a day watching TV and playing video games. That's sad.

Do your son a favor by introducing him to the great outdoors. Throw a ball to one another. Take a bike ride. Explore nature trails. By escaping the allure of digital devices, your son will soon learn that real-life adventure is better than any video game. And when you spend time together, you'll develop memories that will last a lifetime.

CLIMB

HIGHER

When your son gets home from school, what does he do? Does he flop down onto the couch and stare at a screen? How does that affect his physical, mental, and spiritual growth?

What about you? When you get home from work, what do you do? What kind of example are you setting?

‹ **Hawaii** › Located on Hawaii's **Hamakua island**, not far from Kapaau, Palolu Trail rewards hikers with a stunning view of the coast. Though the hike is short, at just under a mile long, one of the main challenges is the sometimes slippery descent into the valley. The climate here is somewhat drier than other parts of Hawaii, but the scenery is no less spectacular. 🚶‍♂️🚶

The Battle for Your Mind

"For though we walk in the flesh, we are not waging war according to the flesh."
— **2 Corinthians 10:3**

26

Boys love battling the bad guys in video games! But did you know an even more ruthless battle rages around your son?

Secular forces are battling for your son's heart and mind. They want to distract him, deceive him, and destroy him by controlling his thoughts. The enemy is clever and deceptive, often using temptation to lure him away from truth. The battle is fierce, and yet, many parents don't even know about the battles their sons are facing.

Fortunately, the Bible provides clear instruction on how to confront the enemy. Romans 12:2 says, "Do not be conformed to this world, but be transformed by the renewal of your mind, that by testing you may discern what is the will of God."

True transformation takes place when we prioritize God in our lives. As a dad, you play a huge role in guiding your son along the pathway of life. Train him to win the battle for his mind by keeping his focus on Christ.

CLIMB HIGHER

Temptation is all around us. Are you successfully battling it?

What practical advice can you give your son about how to achieve victory? What Bible verses would be helpful to memorize?

‹ **VIRGINIA** › **Shenandoah National Park** features some of the most picturesque scenery in northern Virginia with rolling hills, impressive mountains, colorful wildflowers, and spectacular wildlife. The Rose River Trail is a 3.8-mile loop that escorts you along the river with views of the surrounding ridges and Rose River Falls. 🚶🚶

Finding the Right Fit

"Train up a child in the way he should go; even when he is old he will not depart from it." — **Proverbs 22:6**

27

If you plan to go skiing, you wear ski boots. If you're heading to the beach, you wear sandals. For a quick jog around the block, you wear running shoes.

You select your shoes based on the type of activity.

Similarly, when training, correcting, or playing with your son, it's vital to select the appropriate tone for the task at hand. It's also crucial that you understand your son's personality so that you can most effectively connect with him. At times, you may need to choose a serious tone. Other times, a light-hearted attitude is most appropriate.

There's no "one-size-fits-all" type of parenting. That's because dads and sons are each uniquely created by God with their own character traits and temperaments. Understanding your son takes effort. But the more time and attention you devote to him, the more likely he'll respond to your guidance and instruction.

CLIMB HIGHER

Are you contemplative, carefree, or comical? Does your demeanor change when interacting with your son? How could this be positive or negative?

If you have several kids, do you adjust your one-on-one time with them based on their individual interests and personalities? How might guidance to a son look different than instruction to a daughter?

‹ Pennsylvania › Meadow Run Trail, a 3-mile hike, is an excellent way to explore **Ohiopyle State Park** in southwestern Pennsylvania. Youghiogheny River, the trail's main attraction, contains waterfalls, natural water slides, and swimming holes. These features make this state park a fun summer attraction with plenty of places to cool off. 🥾

Lost Expectations

"And we know that for those who love God all things work together for good, for those who are called according to his purpose." — **Romans 8:28**

28

When your son is young, you're filled with dreams of how extraordinary he will eventually become. But if your son has special needs or experiences developmental delays, you dream about him functioning in an ordinary way.

The expectations we have for our children don't always turn out the way we wish. During these times, it's easy to become frustrated, angry, and bitter. We begin questioning God. "Why me? Why did this have to happen to my son?"

When these emotions begin swirling through your mind, return your focus to the God of all comfort. Remember that God selected you as a dad for a specific reason. And because He chose you, He will equip you for the task at hand.

We may never know the reason God allows certain things to happen, but we can—in faith—know that He who began a good work in you (and in your son) will be faithful to complete it (Philippians 1:6).

CLIMB

HIGHER

What expectations for your son haven't come true? How does that make you feel?

Have you committed your son to the Lord to use in whatever way He determines is best?

‹ **Massachusetts** › Located near Plymouth, Massachusetts, the **Myles Standish State Forest** is speckled with sparkling blue ponds amidst an aromatic pine forest. Hikers can reach three ponds in one hike on the College Pond, New Long Pond, and Three Cornered Pond Loop. At only 5.2 miles, this hike is a great way to explore this inviting slice of New England's natural beauty. 🚶🚶

Flying High

"But they who wait for the Lord shall renew their strength; they shall mount up with wings like eagles; they shall run and not be weary; they shall walk and not faint." — **Isaiah 40:31**

29

You've probably never flown an airplane before, but your son might have. Well, not a real airplane, but possibly a Boeing 737 on a video game flight simulator.

When flying, a pilot must rely on his instrument panel for accurate information about airspeed, altitude, and direction. Without this information, the pilot puts himself and his passengers at risk, especially when flying through turbulence and bad weather.

Parenting your son also requires you to rely on important information for a successful journey. This information is found in the Bible.

It's there that God provides wisdom about how your son can develop a trusted flight plan for life—even during the turbulence of his teen years. By following God's instruction manual, dark clouds and swirling winds won't knock your son off course. Instead, he'll be equipped to soar confidently into the future.

CLIMB HIGHER

Are you preparing your son for adulthood? How are you training him today for what he will face tomorrow?

When turbulence arises, how does your son handle the disruption and potential danger? Does he become stressed, or does he rely on the training he has received?

<SOUTH CAROLINA

> Tucked away in South Carolina's Upcountry, **Table Rock State Park** features hiking trails with views of both the rugged Table Rock and the rolling Blue Ridge Mountains visible from its pinnacle. The park's signature trail, Table Rock Trail, is a 6.9-mile hike to the top of Table Rock and back. Plan on making a few stops along the way to check out Carrick Creek Falls and the views from scenic overlooks. 🥾

Lost

"It is the Lord who goes before you. He will be with you; he will not leave you or forsake you. Do not fear or be dismayed."
— **Deuteronomy 31:8**

30

As a kid, did you ever get lost? Maybe it was at a busy mall or at a baseball game. When you realized your parents weren't around, how did that make you feel? Did your heart begin to pound? Did your hands begin to sweat?

It's no fun being lost, so don't put your son in that same position. Train your son about what to do and where to go if he ever finds himself lost in the world. When kids at school want him to do something wrong, how does your son respond? At that moment, does he freeze in indecision? Does he become lost in uncertainty?

The situations that boys encounter in today's anti-Christian culture aren't easy. Peer pressure, gender confusion, and unfamiliar values make many boys feel lost. But they don't have to feel that way. Give your son what he needs to stay grounded in today's unstable world. Help him stay safe and secure by knowing the Rock of our salvation.

CLIMB HIGHER

Does your son know where to find help when feeling lost?

When was the last time you had a "man-to-man" talk with him about how to deal with difficult areas of life?

‹ **GEORGIA** › Nestled in the mountains surrounding the picturesque Bavarian village of Helen, Georgia, **Raven Cliff Falls Trail** is an excellent place to escape into nature and cool off at the falls and creeks running alongside the trail. This hike clocks in at just under 5 miles round trip. Watch your step as you cross over the stones and roots along this popular forest trek.

True Self-Worth

31

"For you formed my inward parts; you knitted me together in my mother's womb. I praise you, for I am fearfully and wonderfully made."
— **Psalm 139:13-14**

Statistics indicate that girls struggle with self-image problems more than boys. But if it's your son that's hurting because he doesn't like how he looks, statistics don't matter. You just want to help your son.

Compounding the problem are social media sites promoting their version of what is physically attractive and culturally trendy. When boys compare themselves with these unrealistic expectations, feelings of inadequacy can cause them to sink into depression.

Help your son develop a proper understanding of true self-worth. Remind him that 1 Peter 2:4 says that in God's sight, we are "chosen and precious."

As you guide your son through life, focus his attention on the Savior, and away from social media sites that batter his self-esteem. By doing so, he'll learn to honor the Lord instead of trying to win the approval of "friends" who aren't really his friends.

CLIMB
HIGHER

What are your son's natural abilities and talents? How can you build up his self-confidence by encouraging him in these activities?

To combat negative influences, what are some healthy outdoor activities you and your son could participate in? (Hint: visit www.TrailLifeUSA.com for a full program of exciting opportunities.)

‹ **OREGON** › South Neahkahnie Mountain Trail, located in **Oswald West State Park**, Oregon, is a 3.4-mile loop through northern Oregon's rugged coastal region. Passing through ferns and evergreen forests, the trail leads hikers to a striking peak with views of the ocean and bay below. Most of the trail is shaded, making it a comfortable place to hike during the summer. 🚶🚶

Grumbles vs. Gratitude

32

"Do all things without grumbling or disputing, that you may be blameless and innocent, children of God without blemish in the midst of a crooked and twisted generation, among whom you shine as lights in the world." — **Philippians 2:14-15**

Does your son ever complain? Most likely, yes.

Perhaps he whines about chores, or having to study for a test, or about what's for dinner. Maybe he complains about not getting the latest digital gadget, or about not being allowed to do a certain activity.

Complaining is almost second nature. However, as a parent, be intentional in teaching your son to focus on the positives of life, rather than on the negatives.

That's tough! But by helping your son follow the Lord, his perspective of what's important in life will change. And as his heart and mind focus on those things that are eternal, the trivial concerns of life will fade away.

But beware. The transformation from grumbling to gratitude isn't quick. It requires a consistent and close relationship with the Lord.

CLIMB HIGHER

When you've had a hard day, how do you respond? Do you complain? Does that help the situation?

It's easy to see weaknesses in people, but showing gratitude requires careful thought and consideration. How could you show gratitude to your son this week?

‹ **OKLAHOMA** › **Beavers Bend State Park** in mountainous southeastern Oklahoma is a gorgeous park highlighted by Broken Bow Lake and the Mountain Fork River. Take a hike along the river on the Friends Trail Loop, a 1.5-mile route not far from the lake. 🚶🚶

Teamwork

"Two are better than one, because they have a good reward for their toil. For if they fall, one will lift up his fellow."
— **Ecclesiastes 4:9-10**

33

Boys love football. Flag football is fun, but when boys reach their teens, tackle football is an even bigger rush.

Quarterbacks and wide receivers get a lot of the glory, but football coaches are quick to point out that it takes an entire team to win a football game.

The same is true in parenting your son.

As a parent, you and your spouse are certainly the most influential people in his life. But his teachers, athletic coaches, and friends also influence his thoughts and actions.

The question is: Are they influencing him to do right? Are they helping him to love the Lord with all his heart, soul, and mind?

If you need some extra teammates to help support you in the game, check out Trail Life USA. Through adventurous outdoor activities, qualified mentors are helping boys learn character, purpose, and leadership. Learn more at TrailLifeUSA.com.

CLIMB HIGHER

It's easy to feel overwhelmed by the demands of life, especially in parenting boys. Do you feel obligated to do everything for your son? Do you feel physically or emotionally stressed?

What areas of life could other people provide you support? How are you being a teammate to other parents?

‹ NEW MEXICO ›

Located just outside of
Santa Fe, the **Jamez
National Recreation
Area** features a sampling
of the dramatic natural
landscapes of northern
New Mexico. The hike to
and from McCauley Hot
Springs from the Jamez
Falls picnic area via the
East Fork Trail is a 3.2-
mile trek showcasing a
clear, natural hot spring
amidst red rocks and
beautiful pine forest. 🚶🚶

Dollars and Sense

"As for the rich in this present age, charge them not to be haughty, nor to set their hopes on the uncertainty of riches, but on God, who richly provides us with everything to enjoy." — 1 Timothy 6:17

34

If you're like most dads, you cringe whenever you have to wait in line at the grocery store. That's because young kids see the checkout aisle as a carnival of possibilities.

"Dad, can I have a candy bar?"

"Not today."

"What about this racecar?"

"No. Put that back."

"Why?"

"Because I said so!"

It's easy to grow frustrated when kids whine for stuff at the store. They're enticed by what they see and they immediately want it.

But use the occasion to teach your son important lessons about financial responsibility. There are many ways to accomplish this, but the ultimate goal is to help your son understand how to manage money, delay gratification, and how to be a good steward of what God has given him.

By training your son in the way he should go, even pennies begin making "sense."

CLIMB HIGHER

When should you begin talking to your son about how to handle money? What will you tell him about what money can and cannot do?

Is your walk consistent with your talk? How do you spend the resources God has entrusted into your care?

‹ **UTaH** › Though an expansive and imposing land-scape, **Zion National Park** in Utah features some highly accessible hikes with unforgettable views. The Zion Canyon Overlook Trail is a 1-mile round-trip which meanders through shady alcoves and up rocky steps until you reach the scenic overlook. 🚶🚶

Strength of Character

35

"Show yourself in all respects to be a model of good works, and in your teaching show integrity, dignity, and sound speech that cannot be condemned . . ."
— **Titus 2:7-8**

Boys love to test their physical strength through competition. This often involves sports such as football, soccer, or wrestling. But boys also measure their strength through weightlifting. By pumping iron, they develop muscle and gain stamina.

The problem is that in the gym, it's easy for boys to think that bigger muscles equal a better man. Teach your son that although lifting dumbbells can produce bigger biceps, even more important than physical strength is strength of character.

Here's an idea. Study Bible characters from God's Word—characters like Joseph, Elijah, and Peter. How did these men succeed or fail in life? What can we learn from their examples?

Becoming a godly man doesn't happen by accident. It takes consistent training. It's fine to use free weights to develop muscle and athletic ability, but make sure you and your son are also exercising godly character.

CLIMB HIGHER

Self-control doesn't come easy for many men and boys. It's a heavy weight to manage. When life doesn't go as planned, how do you exercise patience?

Are you "lifting" your son up in prayer? Are you providing him an example of how a real man of God acts and thinks?

‹ LOUISIANA › Located just a few miles east of Lafayette, Louisiana, the Lake Martin Levee Trail is the perfect place for spotting wildlife, including Herons and Egrets, who use the area as a nesting ground. The 5.1-mile loop meanders through **Cypress Island Preserve**, a swampland full of beautiful Cypress trees and Spanish moss. 🚶🚶

Heroes of the Faith

"Now faith is the assurance of things hoped for, the conviction of things not seen." — **Hebrews 11:1**

36

W ho is your son's hero? Is he a sports star? An actor? A musician?

As you guide your son through today's popstar-infatuated culture, encourage him to study the lives of godly men who displayed courage, service, and devotion.

Introduce your son to heroes of the faith found in Hebrews 11. There he'll learn about ordinary people God used in extraordinary ways. Your son will be captivated when he reads about men who escaped the edge of the sword, endured torture, and were imprisoned for their faith. People like Gideon, Samson, and David. These men weren't perfect. In fact, many of the heroes found in Hebrews 11 made serious mistakes. And yet, God still used them in incredible ways because of their faith in Him.

Living for God isn't easy. But these heroes of the faith remind us that God provides the strength and help to do what is right, even when life is hard.

CLIMB	Who are your heroes? Why do you admire them? Do these people love God and His Word?
HIGHER	Whom does your son admire? Why? Are these people drawing your son toward or away from God? Are there other heroes you could introduce him to?

‹ **Iowa** › **Maquoketa Caves State Park** in Iowa boasts more caves than any other state park in the United States. Whether or not you plan on exploring these caves, hiking the 1.7-mile Maquoketa Caves Loop is an excellent way to experience this remarkable state park. 🚶🚶

Searching for Wisdom

". . . if you seek it [wisdom] like silver and search for it as for hidden treasures, then you will understand the fear of the Lord and find the knowledge of God."
— **Proverbs 2:4-5**

37

When was the last time you went on a scavenger hunt? It seems as if they're making a comeback. Teenagers, especially, like the competitive aspect of searching for and finding a bunch of weird objects, all in the fastest time possible.

Searching for plastic flamingos is hilarious, but don't forget to teach your son about the importance of searching for wisdom in God's Word.

More than ever, today's secular culture tells boys that life is all about fun and pleasure. However, the Bible has a different perspective. It tells us that our ultimate goal is to worship the Lord and serve Him.

Sounds easy enough, but it isn't. That's why it's vital to search the Scriptures for wisdom and instruction—each and every day. In doing so, you'll find the treasure of knowing God more fully and joyfully.

CLIMB HIGHER

How consistent is your time with the Lord? Are the demands of life hurting your spiritual life?

It's important for boys to see their fathers prioritize Bible study and prayer. In addition to that, how can you encourage your own son to search for wisdom?

‹ **NEW YORK** › Hiking to Kaaterskill Falls from the Laurel House Road Trail is a 1.6-mile trek through the **Kaaterskill Wild Forest**. The falls, viewable from a platform at the end of the hike, are the main attraction. This a great way to take in the untamed splendor of upstate New York. 🚶🚶

Generation Z

38

"For we are his workmanship, created in Christ Jesus for good works, which God prepared beforehand, that we should walk in them." — **Ephesians 2:10**

It's likely you've heard about Generation Z. It's a label applied to those born between 1997 and 2012.

Many people look at today's Generation Z as media-obsessed teenagers who are lazy, cynical, and unambitious. But this stereotyping fails to reveal the clever, creative, and compassionate ways these teens are influencing their communities.

Many times, boys simply haven't been inspired to set goals and achieve their dreams. Sometimes they haven't had good role models to push them forward.

William Carey, the father of modern missions, said, "Expect great things from God; attempt great things for God." As a dad, are you helping your son be courageous? Are you helping him develop his potential, passion, and purpose?

While it's commendable to be a success in sports and academics, it's even more important that your son follow the Lord with all his heart, soul, and mind. This will lead him to use his life in an extraordinary way.

CLIMB HIGHER

Are you inspiring your son to achieve worthwhile goals?

What activities could you and your son do that would motivate him to use his energy and creativity for the glory of God?

‹ Maine › Ocean Path Trail in **Acadia National Park** overlooks Maine's Bar Harbor, a popular basecamp for hiking enthusiasts. As you climb 374 feet of elevation along the 4.5-mile trail, you'll enjoy clear views of the rocky coastline. 🥾

Instruction Manual

"Make me to know your ways, O Lord; teach me your paths. Lead me in your truth and teach me, for you are the God of my salvation." — **Psalm 25:4-5**

39

Two simple words strike terror in a parent's heart. Those words are *Assembly Required.*

And yet, too often we ignore the instruction manual when putting together a bike or race car track for our son. We think, "Yeah, I can do this by myself!" But after hours of frustration, we swallow our pride and study the instruction manual to assemble the toy.

Parenting your son is also a complex process, especially these days with so many flashy distractions competing for his attention. The world is trying to yank him toward destructive habits that war against his soul.

Thankfully, God's Word provides detailed instruction on how to guide your son in the way he should go. Take time to read the Book of Proverbs together. There you'll learn practical wisdom about how God wants us to grow and develop throughout life.

CLIMB HIGHER

Being a dad is one thing. Being a dad who guides his son toward biblical maturity is another thing. Are you helping your son become a godly young man?

What influences have the potential of leading your son astray? How can you focus his interests on character-building activities?

‹ Tennessee › Accessing Peregrine Peak via the Alum Cave Bluff Trail is a 4.5-mile hike in **Great Smoky Mountains National Park**, not far from Gatlinburg, Tennessee. Hikers pass under the Alum Cave Bluff on their way to the top of Peregrine Peak, a gradual 1,160-foot ascent. The peak provides an excellent vantage point from which to survey the surrounding mountain landscape. 🚶

Parenting Roller Coaster

"Let me hear in the morning of your steadfast love, for in you I trust. Make me know the way I should go, for to you I lift up my soul." — **Psalm 143:8**

Boys love roller coasters. A popular one at Seaworld Orlando is called Mako. It reaches 200 feet high and races through the air at 73 miles per hour.

That's a crazy ride, but parenting boys can be even more scary—or exciting—depending on how you look at it.

Maybe your son loves spending all the time in the world with you. But then, suddenly, he tapes a sign to his bedroom door that says, "Keep out!" One day he is charming and cute. The next day he's twisting and turning against your rules and authority.

Even when the parenting roller coaster feels out of control, take heart. The Lord has entrusted your son into your care. He knows you are the best person to guide him through life's journey.

Just like a roller coaster, parenting races by in a flash. Despite its ups and downs, take time to enjoy the ride.

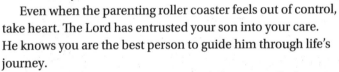

CLIMB HIGHER

Boys have mood swings, but so do dads. What are you doing to create a stable home environment for your son?

When your son goes off the rails, how do you respond? How can you show love while still providing godly correction?

‹ **OREGON** › The Misery Ridge and River Trail cuts through incredible views in Oregon's **Smith Rock State Park**, located 26 miles from Bend. Considered a high-difficulty trail, this 3.6-mile loop passes popular rock climbing sites. As you climb the steep trails, make sure to soak in the sights—from the Crooked River that wanders through the valley to the rugged ridges that tower high above. 🚶🚶

Plagued of Entitlement

41

"For all that is in the world—the desires of the flesh and the desires of the eyes and pride of life—is not from the Father but is from the world." — 1 John 2:16

A horrible plague is sweeping across America, and millions of boys are being infected. This plague is attacking their minds and destroying their ability to live healthy and productive lives.

What is this contagious plague?

It's the disease of entitlement.

More than ever, boys feel entitled to possessions and entertainment. Phrases such as, "I deserve!" and "Give it to me now!" indicate an entitlement attitude.

The tragedy of this mindset is that boys fail to understand that happiness isn't found in the latest digital device, thrilling experience, or trendy amusement. When their minds are focused on themselves and the world's flashy enticements, they're missing out on the joyful life God intended for them.

Don't let the plague of entitlement infect your son. Teach him the value of hard work and contentment. Investing time and attention in your son's mental, social, and spiritual development, you set him up for a healthy and successful life.

CLIMB HIGHER

Does your son have an entitlement attitude, or does he work for the things he wants?

How can you help your son learn contentment in today's materialistic culture?

‹ **WISCONSIN** › The Lost Canyon Trail is a 3.4-mile loop through the **Governor Dodge State Park** near Dodgeville, Wisconsin. About midway through the loop, hikers can enjoy views of the gentle Stephens Falls and a stream winding down to Cox Hollow Lake. 🥾

A Balancing Act

"But seek first the kingdom of God and his righteousness, and all these things will be added to you." — **Matthew 6:33**

42

In the game of Jenga®, the block-stacking game, it's fun taking turns removing blocks while trying to keep the tower intact. But eventually, the tower becomes unbalanced, and the blocks come tumbling down.

As a parent, don't allow yourself to become unbalanced in life. As you go about your daily routines, avoid stacking too many obligations in your life. The higher your number of commitments, the greater the risk of wearing yourself out and having things tumble out of control.

Finding that balance between work and family life can be really hard. The key, though, is determining your priorities and then pursuing those activities that contribute toward your overall goals. But remember, you'll never go wrong by investing time and attention in your son.

CLIMB HIGHER

Are you involved in so many activities that you find yourself darting from one place to another in order to accomplish them all? How do these activities positively or negatively affect your family?

If you stretch yourself too thin, that's unfair to yourself and to your family. Is there one specific activity that isn't the best fit for your life at this time? How could you responsibly remove yourself from that activity?

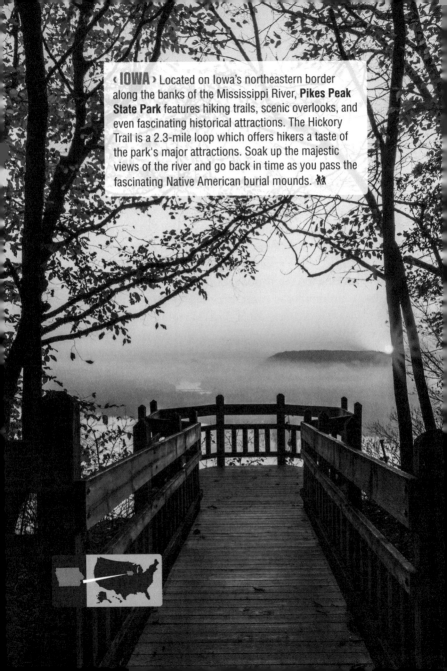

‹ **IOWA** › Located on Iowa's northeastern border along the banks of the Mississippi River, **Pikes Peak State Park** features hiking trails, scenic overlooks, and even fascinating historical attractions. The Hickory Trail is a 2.3-mile loop which offers hikers a taste of the park's major attractions. Soak up the majestic views of the river and go back in time as you pass the fascinating Native American burial mounds. 🚶‍♂️🚶‍♀️

The Great Outdoors

43

"And whatever you do, in word or deed, do everything in the name of the Lord Jesus, giving thanks to God the Father through him."— **Colossians 3:17**

If you've got a boy in your house, you know that God made him with lots of energy and enthusiasm.

That's why it's important that you allow your son to experience fun, excitement, and adventure beyond the everyday routines of life.

This can sometimes be difficult at home where space is limited. But in the great outdoors, there's tons of space and lots of opportunity for exploration and exercise.

Having fun in the backyard or a local park is great, but don't forget to consider outdoor adventures that crank up the adrenaline. This might involve mountain biking, whitewater rafting, or rock climbing.

Even though these types of activities are the exception, you can still make awesome memories that won't break the bank. Consider hiking in a national park or camping out in the forest. Some of the best memories are made while roasting marshmallows around a campfire.

CLIMB HIGHER

When was the last time you took your son on a fun activity? How did he respond?

What's an outdoor activity you could begin planning? How could you use your time during that activity to talk to your son about issues he's facing at school or with his friends?

‹ ILLINOIS › Winding through the heart of **Starved Rock State Park** near Utica, Illinois, the St. Louis Canyon Trail leads hikers to a charming spring-fed waterfall. The 2.1-mile hike is partly paved and features several staircases. Watch your footing but don't forget to keep an eye out for wild turkeys, hawks, foxes, and chipmunks that can sometimes be spotted along the way.

Targeted

44

"Finally, brothers, whatever is true, whatever is honorable, whatever is just, whatever is pure, whatever is lovely, whatever is commendable, if there is any excellence, if there is anything worthy of praise, think about these things." — **Philippians 4:8**

Warning! Your son is being targeted. A relentless enemy is trying to entice, trap, and destroy his heart and mind. This enemy hides in the shadows—yet is constantly attacking your son.

Who is this enemy? It's pornography. The top pornographic website has more visits each day than Netflix, Instagram, and Twitter—combined!

Don't let pornography destroy your son's heart, mind, and future. Help him develop a solid foundation in Scripture. Remind him that Philippians 4:8 instructs him to think on things that are true, honorable, and pure.

It's a tough world out there for boys. That's why it's vital you spend one-on-one time with your son. Guide him in developing godly character that will help him walk worthy of God's calling in his life.

CLIMB HIGHER

Your home should offer safety from the vile sinfulness of the world. And yet, our digital devices often allow the enemy to infiltrate the walls of our home. How are you safeguarding your son's heart and mind?

How are you counter-attacking evil with good? What are some fun, character-building activities you and your son could participate in?

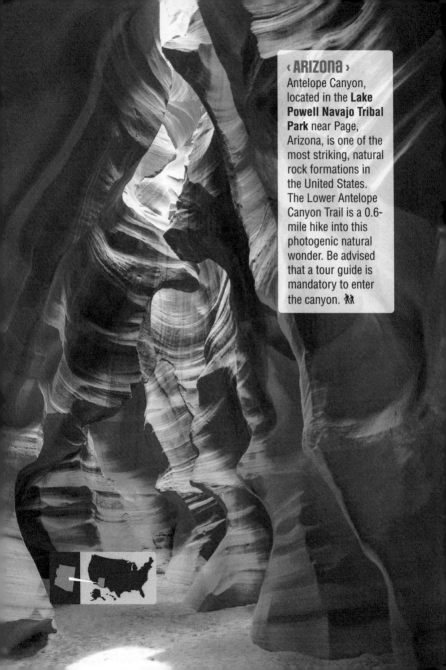

< ARIZONA >

Antelope Canyon, located in the **Lake Powell Navajo Tribal Park** near Page, Arizona, is one of the most striking, natural rock formations in the United States. The Lower Antelope Canyon Trail is a 0.6-mile hike into this photogenic natural wonder. Be advised that a tour guide is mandatory to enter the canyon. 🥾

Friends

"A man of many companions may come to ruin, but there is a friend who sticks closer than a brother."— **Proverbs 18:24**

45

Social media has tremendous power to influence your son's thoughts and actions. But there's an even more influential force in your son's life—and that's his friends.

Research and personal experience tell us that a positive, faith-based environment filled with genuine friends is one of the best ways to shield your son against negative influences. This keeps him accountable and his mind focused on activities that aren't crude and crass.

Though it's unreasonable for you to expect your son's friends to be perfect, they should exhibit a general attitude of respect and obedience to authority. Do you know who your son's friends are? Are they a good influence, or do they display destructive behaviors that could negatively affect him?

By helping your son know how to choose good friends, you provide an atmosphere of growth and development that sets him up for success.

CLIMB HIGHER

Who are your son's three best friends? Do they know the Lord Jesus as their Savior? Do their lives demonstrate a journey of growth?

How could you get to know your son's friends better? What activities could you, your son, and his friends (and maybe their dads as well) all do together that would be fun and character building?

‹ NEW HAMPSHIRE ›

Mount Willard Trail in **White Mountain National Forest** near Bretton Woods, New Hampshire, contains a steep climb but results in astounding views. The 3.1-mile route begins at Saco Lake and guides hikers over rocky terrain. From the trail, you'll see some of the tallest and most scenic mountains on the east coast.

Stand and Salute

"Blessed is the nation whose God is the Lord, the people whom he has chosen as his heritage!" — **Psalm 33:12**

46

When the national anthem is sung or the pledge of allegiance recited, does your son stand and place his right hand over his heart? If he's wearing a hat, does he remove it out of respect?

Since 1777, the American flag has stood as a powerful symbol of liberty and justice. The stars and stripes remind us of the sacrifice that many men and women gave so that we can enjoy this land of the free.

Teach your son the meaning of the flag's colors. White signifies purity and innocence. Red indicates courage. Blue is a sign of perseverance and justice.

Even though the flag is a simple piece of nylon fabric, it represents the history, values, and strength of our great nation. Train your son to stand and salute the flag, and in this way honor our American heritage.

CLIMB HIGHER

Are you teaching your son to appreciate and defend the biblical foundation on which this nation was established?

Saluting the flag is a way of showing respect to our country as well as to all those who have served in the armed forces. When was the last time you thanked a veteran for his or her service? How could you and your son demonstrate this thankfulness in a practical way?

‹ **SOUTH DAKOTA** › The Pinnacles Overlook Trail in **Badlands National Park**, South Dakota, provides excellent views of layered rock formations. At just 0.2 miles, this easy hike offers quick access to incredible views. The overlook is an exceptional spot from which to view sunsets and otherworldly terrain surrounding it. Check out the towering rock formations and raw, rugged landscape extending to the horizon.

Visually Influenced

"The eye is the lamp of the body. So, if your eye is healthy, your whole body will be full of light, but if your eye is bad, your whole body will be full of darkness."
— **Matthew 6:22-23**

47

Boys are influenced by what they see. That's a fact. The question is: What are they looking at throughout the day? According to statistics, the average boy spends hours a day looking at phones, tablets, or other digital devices.

That isn't healthy. But even more disturbing is the realization that online entertainment is bombarding boys with sensual and even pornographic images.

Guys may think they're tough, but they're no match against sexual temptation. A recent study found that 90% of teens have watched porn by age 18. Those images are destroying their ability to form lasting relationships—including a proper relationship with the Lord.

Talking about sex with your son might be one of the hardest things you ever have to do. But if you don't talk about it, your son may be swallowed up by the flood of secular voices bombarding him on his phone. Guide him in the way he should go. He's worth it.

CLIMB HIGHER

When was the last time you had a heart-to-heart talk with your son about how to resist temptation?

What's your son watching on his phone? Have you installed filtering software on all digital devices (including yours)?

‹ **OHIO** › What could be more Ohioan than a buckeye? The hike from Upper Falls to Lower Falls via the Buckeye Trail is a popular 1.2-mile loop offering hikers a good look at some of the waterfalls and rock formations that characterize Ohio's **Hocking Hills State Park**. Because many of the trails in the park are one-way, double check that you are entering the loop at the correct point before setting out. 🚶

Sibling Rivalry

48

"If anyone says, 'I love God,' and hates his brother, he is a liar; for he who does not love his brother whom he has seen cannot love God whom he has not seen."
— 1 John 4:20

God made boys with a competitive spirit. They crave the excitement of challenging themselves against others and emerging victorious.

This desire to compete is a positive characteristic. But when competition within the home transforms into sibling rivalry, beware.

Sibling rivalry often begins with jealousy before mutating into resentment and bitterness. Because brothers and sisters don't know how to process these emotions, they often resort to bickering, insults, and even outright fighting.

As a parent, it's easy to grow impatient with your quarreling kids. Instead, take time to pray for wisdom. Evaluate what the core issue is and then respond accordingly.

Many times, boys simply need to get outside and exercise more. They need an outlet for their competitive spirit. As a dad, be strategic in directing their energy into character-building sports and other activities that will benefit them now and in years to come.

CLIMB HIGHER

Today's culture rewards participation, regardless of achievement. But real life doesn't work that way. When your son fails a test or doesn't win on the ball field, how do you respond? How can a proper response lead to growth?

‹ **NORTH CAROLINA** › Located in the heart of **Pisgah National Forest** near Montreat, North Carolina, Point Lookout Trail is a 7.2-mile hike with great views of the surrounding ridges and mountains. The trail is paved at the beginning and mostly shaded, but you'll be challenged by the uphill hike on the second leg of the journey. Keep your eyes peeled for wildlife and soak up God's craftsmanship in this beautiful national forest. 🥾

Take Time to Rest

49

"Come to me, all who labor and are heavy laden, and I will give you rest."
— **Matthew 11:28**

Being a parent is one of the greatest joys in life. It's also exhausting!

Whether it seems like you've changed a million diapers or whether you feel like a professional taxi driver for your kids, each age and stage of life has its own challenges.

As a dad, it's certainly your responsibility to guide and train your children. But it's also important for you to take time to rest physically, emotionally, and spiritually. Even the Lord Jesus needed to be refreshed. He took time away from his earthly ministry to pray and regain His strength. What a great example for us to follow.

Remember, you don't have to be superhuman to be a super dad. Instead, by taking time to study the Bible and by seeking God's help for day-to-day decisions, you'll be more ready and more motivated to serve the Lord and your family with all your heart, soul, and mind.

CLIMB HIGHER

Are you taking time to rest? How are you doing this physically, emotionally, and spiritually?

Have you set up boundaries to help control your time and priorities? This might look like no phone, TV, or other work activities after a certain time at night. By setting boundaries, you show your son what a balanced lifestyle looks like.

‹ **Tennessee** › **Prentice Cooper State Park** sprawls across Signal Mountain, towering above Chattanooga, Tennessee. Edward's Point Trail, a 3.8-mile hike, offers a vantage point from which hikers can watch the Tennessee River weave its way through the mountains. The journey there and back from Edward's Point is quite memorable as well, featuring a suspension bridge, waterfall, and plenty of interesting rock formations. 🚶🚶

Run the Race

"Let us also lay aside every weight, and sin which clings so closely, and let us run with endurance the race that is set before us, looking to Jesus, the founder and perfecter of our faith." —**Hebrews 12:1-2**

50

Do you like to run? Most people don't. To excel, the sport requires training, endurance, and determination.

In some ways, parenting is a lot like running a race. But the parenting race is more similar to a half marathon than a sprint. When our boys are young, we feel as if we're constantly correcting them. We wonder, "Will this ever end?"

But before you know it, you've rounded the corner and face your son's teen years. During this stretch of the race, you encounter new hurdles, challenges, and obstacles. Exhaustion tries to slow you down. Discouragement tries to trip you up.

Regardless of where you're at in the parenting race, don't quit! Because the Lord entrusted you with parenting your son, He will provide you strength along the way.

So keep on running. You can victoriously finish the race!

CLIMB HIGHER

How's your parenting race going? Have you figured out your stride?

Comparison is a dangerous pothole that can trip you up. That's why it's important to realize that everyone runs differently. Are you running the race God has set out for you?

‹ **COLORADO** › A 2.5-hour drive west of Denver, Colorado, brings you to **White River National Forest**. Once there, check out the 3.1-mile Hanging Lake Trail. It's particularly famous for incredible views along the way to the lake. The steep, mountain hike features a series of bridges. Note that the city of Glenwood Springs requires a permit to hike to the falls. For more information, see visitglenwood.com. 🚶

Fixing a Flat

51

"Let all bitterness and wrath and anger and clamor and slander be put away from you, along with all malice. Be kind to one another, tenderhearted, forgiving one another, as God in Christ forgave you." — Ephesians 4:31-32

If your car has a flat tire, it's important to fix it fast. If you keep driving on it, the rim will shred the rubber. After that you'll ruin the alignment, brakes, and suspension. You might even lose control of the vehicle.

Similarly, if your relationship with your son is deflated, it's important to fix it fast. Maybe you had a disagreement or misunderstanding with him. Maybe harsh words were said. Maybe impatience won the day.

Regardless of who was at fault, it's important to patch things up. This requires humility, communication, and a whole lot of prayer. It also requires a willingness to forgive and forget. But don't delay. You don't want bitterness causing more serious problems down the road.

Repairing a flat relationship (and engaging in preventative maintenance) will go a long way in helping you and your son go the distance.

CLIMB HIGHER	It's hard for guys to say, "I'm sorry." It feels like failure. And yet, we all make mistakes. When a wrong has been committed, a mature person asks for forgiveness. When was the last time you apologized? What was the result?

‹ NORTH DAKOTA › The Petrified Forest to Overlook Trail in **Theodore Roosevelt National Park** offers hikers a memorable encounter with the legendary North Dakota Badlands. At 5.1 miles, the trail is a rewarding journey for those seeking an extended hike. With 469 feet of elevation gain, hikers should expect steep sections that add a touch of challenge to the adventure. 🚶🚶

Smile

"A glad heart makes a cheerful face . . ."
— **Proverbs 15:13**

Do you ever use the smiley emoji 😊 while texting? That emoji helped launch World Smile Day, which is celebrated the first Friday in October. On that day, people are encouraged to smile at people around them.

Fortunately, you don't need an official holiday to smile. It's something you can do every day. Of course, life doesn't always run smoothly. Health issues, work conflicts, and financial stress may catch you off guard. Your furnace or air conditioner may need repair. Or perhaps your son breaks one of the rules you've set in place for his own good.

When these things happen, it's normal for a smile to transform into a frown. You don't have to be happy about hardship and headaches, but you can keep them in proper perspective. Because God is in control of all things, you can rely on Him to carry you through.

So smile! 😊 Not only will a smile help lower your stress level, but it'll also show your son that God's grace provides lasting peace. That's definitely something you can smile about.

CLIMB	Do your facial expressions convey the joy of the Lord? Would your son characterize your normal, everyday attitude as grumpy or gracious?
HIGHER	How do you have fun? What makes your son laugh? Are you giving your time and energy to bringing a smile to his face?

‹ **ARKANSAS** › Whitaker Point Trail (also known as Hawksbill Crag Trail) is a 2.7-mile trek through the **Ozark National Forest** near Pettigrew, Arkansas. The trail is cradled under a canopy of trees, giving way to a clearing as you approach Hawksbill Crag. Take in the breathtaking views of the rolling hills before heading back to the trailhead.

Consequences

"Do not be deceived: God is not mocked, for whatever one sows, that will he also reap." — **Galatians 6:7**

I f your son is like most boys, he's curious and spontaneous. These characteristics help boys better understand the world around them. They climb trees, explore woods, and collect bugs (until Mom finds out).

Being inquisitive is fine, but when excitement is not properly controlled—impulsive actions can lead to problems and pain.

Help your son understand that actions have consequences. A great way to do this is to read the Bible with him. Point out that Moses faithfully served God, but because he disobeyed in providing water to the Israelites, he was not allowed to enter the promised land. Show him how Samson thought he was invincible, but that he was no match against Delilah. Talk about how Peter thought he could walk on water, but that he sank when he took his eyes off Jesus.

By studying good and bad examples of human behavior, your son will gain a better understanding of how to act with discernment and wisdom.

CLIMB HIGHER

When your son disobeys, are there consequences? What happens if you threaten consequences but don't enforce them?

We often think of consequences as being negative, but consequences can also be positive. How can you use consequences to reward good behavior or to celebrate achievement?

‹ **Alabama** › Located just a few miles east of Huntsville, Alabama, **Monte Sano State Park** provides hikers with easy access to magnificent views of the surrounding countryside. The North Plateau Loop, a 2-mile hike, offers access to Logan Point, a scenic overlook. 🚶🚶

Biblical Masculinity

*"Let no one despise you for your youth,
but set the believers an example in speech,
in conduct, in love, in faith, in purity."*
— 1 Timothy 4:12

54

What does it mean to be a man? Does it mean acting macho or being able to bench press 200 pounds? Does it mean reaching a certain age, having a certain number of kids, or accomplishing something prestigious?

Today's anti-Christian culture often idolizes men who are stylish, popular, and rich. But being a man involves so much more.

Qualities of biblical masculinity include courage, service, leadership, sacrifice, commitment, self-control, and unconditional love.

The Apostle Paul encouraged Timothy to set a godly example through his character and conduct. And as dads, we should do the same thing. We should demonstrate—through action—how to be a man that loves God, loves his family, and loves to serve the Lord.

CLIMB HIGHER

Are you teaching your son the characteristics of a godly man? How specifically are you doing that?

Today's culture views humility as weakness. But what does the Bible say about this? Read Proverbs 11:2, Luke 14:11, and James 3:13 with your son. Discuss what those verses teach us about how to interact with one another.

‹ **Texas** › Just north of Fredericksburg, Texas, **Enchanted Rock** is a mesmerizing sight, especially if you catch it at sunrise or sunset. The Enchanted Rock Loop, within the Enchanted Rock State Natural Area, is a memorable 5.4-mile excursion featuring intriguing rock formations, rolling hills, and a variety of wildlife. 🚶‍♂️

Parenting Teen Boys

"God is our refuge and strength, a very present help in trouble. Therefore we will not fear . . ." — **Psalm 46:1-2**

Parenting boys is tough. Parenting teenage guys is 100 times tougher! Or at least it can feel like it.

When your teenage son challenges your authority, when he blatantly disobeys, or when he rolls his eyes at your advice—it's natural to feel frustrated. It's easy to think, "Why me? Why do I have a son that acts like this?"

In these moments of crisis, take heart. Remember that the Lord makes no mistakes.

In His divine wisdom, the Lord chose you to be your son's parent. That's a tremendous responsibility. And because the Lord called you to this important task, He will continue to equip and strengthen you for the job.

CLIMB HIGHER

Does your son's behavior make you want to pull out your hair? When you feel stressed, what do you do? Are you relying on the Lord . . . or your own strength?

Raising teenage boys isn't easy. Fortunately, you're not alone. The church and other Christian organizations can provide help and resources. However, if you need help, are you willing to ask for it?

‹ **ALASKA** › Iditarod Trail to **Rapid's Yurt** near Anchorage, Alaska, is a beautiful hike with a scenic view of Pleasant Mountain. This trail was formerly used as part of the Iditarod, an annual 1,100-mile dog sled race. Unlike the dog sled race route, however, this hike is only 3.8 miles, perfect for a brisk day-hike in the rugged Alaskan mountains. 🚶🚶

Seasons of Change

"For everything there is a season, and a time for every matter under heaven."
— **Ecclesiastes 3:1**

I f you live in the north, the transition from one season to the next brings dramatic weather changes. Many people enjoy the coolness of fall, but winter quickly pushes those mild temperatures away. By the time February rolls around, people yearn for the warmth of spring, but that's soon replaced by the blazing heat of summer.

Seasons are a natural part of our environment. So are the seasons of our children's lives.

As parents, we sometimes wish we could hold back time and keep our kids longer during a specific season of development. Maybe you loved those days when you held your son's hand as he learned to walk. Or perhaps you wish for a return to those days when you could help him with his math homework—those grade school days before he started algebra.

It's fine to remember moments from the past, but don't let that stop you from enjoying the present. Now is the time to continue making memories as you guide your son in transitioning from one season to the next, from one area of growth to the next.

CLIMB HIGHER

Because growth often occurs a little at a time, we don't see it dramatically occurring. Yet it's important to recognize that it's still happening. In what ways is your son growing? How do you acknowledge growth and praise his achievements?

‹ **MICHIGAN** › The hike to Mosquito Falls and Chapel Falls via Chapel Loop in **Pictured Rocks National Lakeshore**, Michigan, is a captivating adventure that showcases the area's natural wonders. The 10.2-mile trail provides hikers the opportunity to explore the extensive and diverse landscape. This moderately challenging hike features 754 feet of elevation gain, with some difficult sections that lead to rewarding viewpoints and cascading waterfalls. 🚶🚶

Conquering Giants

57

"Then David said to the Philistine, 'You come to me with a sword and with a spear and with a javelin, but I come to you in the name of the Lord . . . For the battle is the Lord's, and he will give you into our hand.'" — **1 Samuel 17:45, 47**

Boys love the story of David and Goliath. After all, anytime there's a battle involving giants with swords, it's sure to capture attention.

But too often, boys fail to apply important lessons from David's life. Before David defeated Goliath, he had learned to depend on God when battling lions that attacked his sheep. By relying on God in these smaller tests of faith, David had confidence that God would help him no matter what giant situation came his way.

The more your son understands that true strength comes from God—for both the big and small stuff—the more victorious he will be in life.

CLIMB HIGHER

Giants come in all shapes and sizes. They may be physical, mental, or emotional. What giants is your son facing? At school, is he struggling academically? Does he know how to navigate peer pressure? Is he tempted to watch inappropriate videos?

How are you helping your son conquer giants? How can he move forward in life with greater confidence?

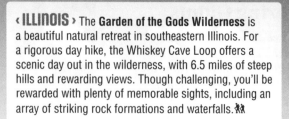

‹ ILLINOIS › The **Garden of the Gods Wilderness** is a beautiful natural retreat in southeastern Illinois. For a rigorous day hike, the Whiskey Cave Loop offers a scenic day out in the wilderness, with 6.5 miles of steep hills and rewarding views. Though challenging, you'll be rewarded with plenty of memorable sights, including an array of striking rock formations and waterfalls. 🥾🥾

3, 2, 1 . . . Lift Off!

"For I know the plans I have for you, declares the Lord, plans for welfare and not for evil, to give you a future and a hope." — **Jeremiah 29:11**

58

There's a bunch of excitement in the rocket industry. NASA, SpaceX, and other companies are building gigantic rockets. They're even planning missions to Mars.

But before a rocket ever leaves the ground, there are countless hours of construction and programming. Every part of the rocket is checked and double-checked to make sure it's ready for liftoff.

Before your son heads off for college or moves away for work, it's important to prepare him for that big day. Make sure he has everything he needs to accomplish the mission of honoring the Lord with his life. This includes carrying with him important characteristics such as honesty, respect, and a strong work ethic.

Of course, becoming a young man of God doesn't happen instantly. That building process begins years before liftoff. Carefully and strategically train your son when he is young. That way, when he is ready to launch out into the world, his mission in life will be a success.

CLIMB HIGHER

Launch day will be here before you know it. How are you preparing your son for that big event?

What biblical characteristics do you consider especially important? In what ways are you helping your son learn these?

‹ **OKLAHOMA** › Dripping Springs Trail, a favorite hiking spot in **Natural Falls State Park**, near Colcord, Oklahoma, is a 1.1-mile loop which shows off the park's 77-foot water-fall. Meandering alongside the creek, the trail is shaded and paved, making it a comfortable way to experience some remarkable scenery. 🏃🏃

What a Privilege

"The father of the righteous will greatly rejoice; he who fathers a wise son will be glad in him." — **Proverbs 23:24**

59

Billy Graham was one of the most influential evangelists of the 20th century. He boldly proclaimed the Gospel to over 200 million people. But in addition to his important preaching ministry, Billy Graham also had an important message for fathers.

He said, "A good father is one of the most unsung, unpraised, unnoticed, and yet one of the most valuable assets in our society."

As a dad, you have the incredible privilege of raising your son to love the Lord and follow His ways. This brings with it the responsibility of providing a strong, Christ-centered foundation for your family.

So, how is your parenting journey coming along? Where are you experiencing successes? What areas do you need to work on?

Being a dad is a privilege as well as a responsibility. It comes with highs and lows. But when you remember that you are investing in eternal souls, your time and effort will always be worth it.

CLIMB
_____
HIGHER

Today's culture ridicules dads. They're portrayed as mindless jocks that don't care about anyone but themselves. Your actions, however, set an example to your son. Are you showing your son how a real man of God talks and acts?

‹ **IDAHO** › **Payette National Forest** is a great place to encounter the remote natural beauty of central Idaho. The Boulder Lake Loop is a 6.4-mile hike which leads hikers past vibrant blue lakes and over a series of wooded ridges. The view of Louie Lake, with a snow-capped peak as its backdrop, is particularly picturesque. 🚶

Broken No More

"May the God of endurance and encouragement grant you to live in such harmony with one another . . ."
— **Romans 15:5**

60

Have you ever broken an arm? Depending on the type of break, the doctor might have needed to set the bones straight before placing your arm in a cast. That cast kept your arm protected so that the broken bones could grow back together.

Relationships can also break, and those breaks are sometimes even more painful than a broken arm.

If your relationship with your son is broken, you need to set things straight as soon as possible. After that, take time to allow the relationship to heal. This may require a season of rest and extra attention. You may need to cut out other activities so that you can devote extra time to helping the relationship recover.

A broken relationship hurts. But by taking immediate steps to help it recuperate, you and your son will grow closer together, and—in time—stronger than ever.

CLIMB HIGHER

Most guys prefer not to talk about broken relationships. They would rather ignore the problem and hope it goes away. But ignoring hurt and pain isn't a solution. If you and your son have had a disagreement or conflict, what steps can you take to mend the relationship?

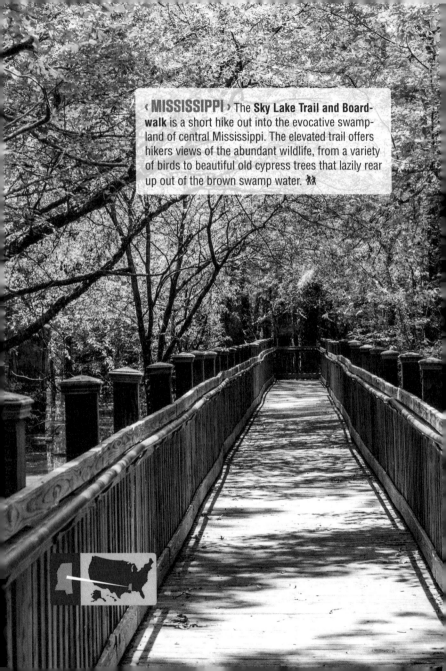

‹ **MISSISSIPPI** › The **Sky Lake Trail and Boardwalk** is a short hike out into the evocative swampland of central Mississippi. The elevated trail offers hikers views of the abundant wildlife, from a variety of birds to beautiful old cypress trees that lazily rear up out of the brown swamp water. 🚶🚶

Step by Step

". . . walk in a manner worthy of the call-
ing to which you have been called, with
all humility and gentleness, with patience,
bearing with one another in love."
— **Ephesians 4:1-2**

D o you remember your son taking his first steps? No doubt you had already been holding his hand and helping him take one step in front of the other. Eventually, though, the day came when he climbed to a stand and took those first few steps all by himself. You took video of him wobbling forward as you cheered with joy and excitement.

Even though your son is no longer a toddler, continue to train him to walk in righteousness. Psalm 1 provides excellent instruction. It teaches us to avoid walking in the counsel of the wicked. This means not being influenced by worldly philosophies that conflict with biblical truth. Instead, we should study God's Word for guidance on how to conduct ourselves while still loving the lost and helping them understand the way to salvation.

Training your son doesn't happen quickly. But like anything worth doing, the more time and effort you put into it, the better the results.

CLIMB
HIGHER

Are you walking worthy of God's call in your life? Are you actively relying on God to be the best dad you can be?

‹ **MICHIGAN** › The Empire Bluff Trail in **Sleeping Bear Dunes National Lakeshore** offers a gorgeous view of Lake Michigan. The trail, located near Empire, Michigan, is 1.5 miles long with 170 feet of elevation gain. While the view alone is well worth the short trek up the bluff, hikers will also appreciate the colorful wildflowers sprinkled throughout the beech-maple forest. 🥾

A Lighthouse in Life

62

"You are the light of the world. A city set on a hill cannot be hidden. In the same way, let your light shine before others, so that they may see your good works and give glory to your Father who is in heaven." — Matthew 5:14, 16

Here's a trivia question: Which state has the most lighthouses? If you answered Michigan, you're absolutely right.

In the darkness of night, lighthouses warn sailors of shallow sandbars and rocky shorelines. Without these lighthouses, many boats and sailors would crash into these obstacles and suffer hardship and pain.

In many ways, you serve as a lighthouse to your son. As he sails through life, you are in a key position to warn him of unseen hazards. Help him avoid the sweeping currents of worldly philosophies, the razor-sharp rocks of peer pressure, and the riptides of raunchy social media sites.

Use your own personal experiences to point your son in the right direction. But make sure you also emphasize the importance of God's Word. The Bible offers him the best practical guidance in navigating the seas of life.

CLIMB HIGHER

Even though your son faces a whole bunch of issues you didn't encounter when you were a kid, you can still help him stay on course. Are you taking the time to do this?

‹ **NEBRASKA** › Smith Falls Trail, near Sparks, Nebraska, is a 1.1-mile hike to **Smith Falls**, a beautiful waterfall tucked away near the wooded banks of the Niobrara River. The trail features a charming bridge and viewing platform directly in front of the falls. 🥾

Puzzle Pieces

"Wait for the Lord; be strong, and let your heart take courage; wait for the Lord!"
— **Psalm 27:14**

How do you feel about puzzles?

When putting together a 500 or 1,000-piece puzzle, you don't normally complete it all at one time. You work on it for a few minutes here and a few minutes there. Some people like to start with the corners and edges. Other people assemble the puzzle based on color or pattern.

Regardless of what puzzle-building technique you use, the pieces start coming together until—at long last— you see the entire puzzle in all its glory.

Too often, we expect our sons to mature faster than what is realistic. We wish to see the entire picture of his youth from the very start, but the growth process doesn't work that way.

God's picture for your son's life is assembled one piece at a time. Clear communication fits into instruction. Correction fits into responsibility. Quality time fits into encouragement and trust.

As you rely on God for guidance, He will transform the pieces of your son's life into a beautiful masterpiece.

CLIMB HIGHER

How can you demonstrate patience to your son even when his attitudes and behavior puzzle you? What illustration from your own life could you use to connect with him?

‹ **ARIZONA** › **Saguaro National Park**, located just outside of Tucson, Arizona, features miles of trails through one of the nation's most iconic terrains. Bridal Wreath Falls Trail is a 5.7-mile out-and-back hike through the beautiful Sonoran Desert landscape, famous for its Wild West associations and striking Saguaro cacti. 🚶🚶

Slow and Steady

"But grow in the grace and knowledge of our Lord and Savior Jesus Christ."
— 2 Peter 3:18

64

The saguaro cactus is an amazing desert plant. It stretches high into the air like a telephone pole, reaching heights of 40 feet or more.

But did you know that this colossal cactus grows slowly? It isn't unusual for it to be 2-inches tall on its 10th birthday. Soon after, the saguaro begins growing faster and keeps up this steady growth until eventually towering over other cacti species.

Maybe your son is like the saguaro. Maybe he's a slow learner at school. Sure, it's fine to get him extra tutoring help, but it's important to realize that we all have different rates of physical, mental, and spiritual growth. The key is to continue growing—little by little and day by day.

The saguaro cactus starts growing slowly. But in the end, it towers strong and tall. So can your son.

CLIMB HIGHER

Even if your teen son has reached his adult height, he isn't done growing in other ways. If he seems prickly at times, he may just need more time to bloom. What age-appropriate activities will help nourish his growth?

How can he develop a deep-rooted foundation in Christ that will help him reach his potential?

‹ **Alaska** › The Savage Alpine Trail cuts through the mythical landscape of Alaska's **Denali National Park**. Surrounded by jagged, snow-capped mountains jutting out of the alpine tundra, this 4.1-mile trail is perfect for those looking for a strenuous and scenic adventure. Because of the slippery ice and remote location, hikers should make sure to have proper equipment before embarking on this trek. 🥾

Walking a Tightrope

"I have set the Lord always before me; because he is at my right hand, I shall not be shaken." — **Psalm 16:8**

65

How's your balance? And I'm not talking about your checkbook!

In June of 2012, Nik Wallenda walked from the United States' side of Niagara Falls to the Canadian side, high above the raging waterfalls on a 2-inch tightrope!

Gusts of wind and swirling spray made the 1,800-foot crossing physically and mentally exhausting.

At times, parents feel almost as much stress as a daredevil on a tightrope. We have to balance jobs and home responsibilities with our children's academic studies, sports programs, and other activities.

When you start feeling off balance, remember Proverbs 16:3. It says, "Commit your work to the Lord, and your plans will be established." Take one task at a time while keeping your eyes focused on God. After that, leave the results in His capable hands.

CLIMB HIGHER

Parenting kids is a balancing act. You want to demonstrate joy but also need to provide correction. You want to show compassion but also need to emphasize consequences. In what ways is the balancing act of parenting especially challenging for you?

What steps can you take to make life's balancing act more stable?

‹ **NEW JERSEY** › New Jersey's **Worthington State Forest** features striking scenery with commanding views of the Delaware River. Mount Tammany's Red Dot and Blue Dot Loop is a challenging 3.6-mile hike popular for the views it offers of the Delaware Water Gap. 🏃

Let's Talk

". . . let every person be quick to hear, slow to speak, slow to anger." — **James 1:19**

66

Is your cell phone within reach right now? It probably is.

The first cell phone weighed 2.4 pounds and was as big as your head! Fortunately, today's cell phones are much smaller and lighter. They allow us to easily talk and text each other.

And yet, despite the extraordinary technology within a cell phone, these devices often hinder communication. You've seen it—family members sitting beside one another staring at their phones. We're so plugged into these devices that we lose contact with real-life human beings, the very reason why phones were created.

Don't let that be you. Sure, go ahead and use technology, but don't let it replace one-on-one communication. The more you talk and laugh with your son, the more he'll want to put down his phone and share life together with you.

CLIMB HIGHER

Do you spend more time with your son or with your phone? When you're having dinner with the family and your phone rings, do you prioritize your family or the phone call?

It's easy to become addicted to technology. How do you keep that from happening? How can you use digital devices to bring your family closer together?

‹ **SOUTH CAROLINA** ›

Nestled in South Carolina's **Sumter National Forest**, Yellow Branch Falls Trail showcases one of the most spectacular waterfalls in the region. The hike is considered moderately challenging and clocks in at 3.1 miles, there and back. At 50 feet tall, Yellow Branch Falls are a sight to behold, but be sure to watch your step as the trail and rocks can be slippery. 🥾

Strike It Rich

67

"Do not lay up for yourselves treasures on earth, where moth and rust destroy and where thieves break in and steal, but lay up for yourselves treasures in heaven … For where your treasure is, there your heart will be also." — **Matthew 6:19-21**

During the California Gold Rush of 1849, thousands of prospectors panned for gold in mountain streams and riverbeds. But those prospectors who spent time, sweat, and effort digging into the earth were the ones most likely to strike it rich. Discovering a single vein of gold was worth way more than hundreds of gold flakes from the river.

Help your son strike it rich in terms of godly character. Show him—through personal example—how to dig deep into Scripture. It's there that he'll discover the incredible treasures of service, commitment, and integrity.

Remember, the more your son understands the value of honoring the Lord with his life, the more he'll want to store up treasures in heaven—where thieves will never break in and steal.

CLIMB HIGHER

Does your son see you reading and studying God's Word? When was the last time you memorized a Bible verse?

If your son is young, help him learn the books of the Bible. A great way to do this is through fun sword drills. What other ways can you make understanding the Bible fun and practical?

‹ RHODE ISLAND › **The Cliff Walk** in Newport, Rhode Island, is one of the most popular walking routes in the state for good reason. This 7-mile, paved hike straddles the coast on one side and elegant mansions and meticulously manicured gardens on the other. 🚶‍♀️

Our Anchor in a Storm

"He who dwells in the shelter of the Most High will abide in the shadow of the Almighty. I will say to the Lord, 'My refuge and my fortress, my God, in whom I trust.'" — **Psalm 91:1-2**

A furious storm rages around us. Today's anti-Christian culture is battering all those who stand in its way. And it's only getting worse.

Public schools relentlessly attack biblical truth. A progressive wave distorts gender differences. Secular ideology promotes moral relativism.

In this antagonistic society, it's easy for Christian boys to get swept away by confusion and chaos. Plus, they have to withstand the whirlwind of peer pressure, sexual temptation, and greed.

Don't let these weights catch your son off guard and drown him in addiction. Despite today's ungodly cultural current, teach him to stay anchored to the Rock of his salvation. This is done by studying the Bible to know what is true, honorable, and just (Philippians 4:8).

In today's swirling storm of bad influences, your son needs positive role models. Are you demonstrating daily faith in God? Is this evident in your words and actions?

CLIMB HIGHER

How can you help your son discern what is right from what is wrong?

What activities is he involved in that could sink his faith? What activities could help buoy him up spiritually?

‹ **ARKANSAS** › On the outskirts of Little Rock, Arkansas, **Pinnacle Mountain State Park** offers great hiking trails and commanding views of the surrounding landscape. The Pinnacle Mountain West Summit Trail is a challenging, 1.4-mile round-trip hike showcasing the mountaintop views which make this park popular with the locals. 🚶🚶

Packing List

"Make every effort to supplement your faith with virtue, and virtue with knowledge, and knowledge with self-control, and self-control with steadfastness, and steadfastness with godliness."
— **2 Peter 1:5-6**

Ah, vacation! It provides time away from the normal, everyday routines of life.

But before leaving on your last vacation, you probably spent time thinking about what clothes and other items you'd need at your destination. Then you gathered all those things together and packed them into a suitcase.

On this journey called parenthood, it's even more important to bring everything necessary. Begin by packing love. Next, fold in joy. After that, squeeze in humor, laughter, and a bunch of fun. And, of course, don't forget to include patience, gratitude, and forgiveness.

Make sure you come up with your own packing list as you journey through the hills and valleys of parenthood. Having these virtues with you will make the ups and downs much more manageable.

CLIMB HIGHER

The Bible provides a big "packing list" of qualities that we need. Even though this list is intimidating, we need to remember that developing godly character is a process. How are you growing closer to the Lord from week to week?

How does a stronger walk with the Lord lead to a stronger walk with your son?

‹ **Nevada** › Monkey Rock Trail in the **Humboldt-Toiyabe National Forest** in central Nevada is memorable for its panoramic views of Lake Tahoe as well as for its granite Monkey Rock formation. Because this 2.6-mile trail gains 498 of elevation, be ready for some cardio, especially if you're not used to high-altitude hiking. 🏃🏃

Instant Replay

"But one thing I do: forgetting what lies behind and straining forward to what lies ahead." — **Philippians 3:13b**

Boys love football. And these days, a great benefit of watching football on TV is the instant replay. You can re-watch—and practically relive—those exciting catches, fumbles, and interceptions.

The instant replay is fantastic, but in real life, there is no "redo." You get only one chance to raise your son through his adolescent years.

But what if you haven't trained your son as well as you wish you had? If that's the case, take heart. C.S. Lewis said, "You can't go back and change the beginning, but you can start where you are and change the ending."

As a parent, you don't get to redo your son's youth. You may wish you could go back and be there for him during the big game or during an important performance. But the fact is, you can't.

However, you can be more attentive, compassionate, and involved in the future. There's still time to make each play count so that in the end, you score a win for the glory of God.

CLIMB HIGHER

It's easy to look back and see parenting failures. But remember: You can still make a difference in your son's life. How do you plan on tackling that challenge?

‹ **Minnesota** › Hidden right in the heart of Minneapolis, Minnesota, the **Minnehaha Falls** Loop provides fast access to natural scenery. Despite the trail being only 0.8 miles long, hikers will enjoy walking along the peaceful Minnehaha Creek and taking time to stand in awe of the majestic Minnehaha Falls. 🏃🏃

He Is No Fool

"For whoever would save his life will lose it, but whoever loses his life for my sake will find it." — **Matthew 16:25**

71

I n 1956, Jim Elliot was murdered by tribesmen in the jungles of Ecuador. Newspaper reporters wondered why this missionary would risk his life for uncivilized people. Though Jim Elliot died at only 28 years old, he had a proper perspective of life. He said, "He is no fool who gives what he cannot keep to gain what he cannot lose."

Too often, we hold tightly to possessions and activities that hold no eternal value. While they may not be wrong in themselves, keep their importance in proper perspective. Don't make the mistake of clinging to things of insignificance.

As a dad, are you teaching your son to give his time and talents to worthwhile causes? This is best demonstrated through action. What activities are you involved in that are making a difference in people's lives? If you've been living for self, now is the time to turn that around. As you make God a daily priority, your possessions and activities will come into proper focus.

CLIMB HIGHER — What's your most prized possession? Did you immediately think about a physical object or your family? Are you hanging on to worldly things too tightly?

‹ **MARYLAND** › **Assateague Island** lies off of the Maryland coast, serving as the eastern edge of Chincoteague Bay. This lovely island is home to wild horses, beaches, and a variety of biking and walking paths. Woodland Bivalve Trail is a 2.1-mile loop that covers the sandy, wooded terrain and offers breathtaking views of the Atlantic. 🚶🚶

Renewing Your Mind

72

"Do not be conformed to this world, but be transformed by the renewal of your mind, that by testing you may discern what is the will of God, what is good and acceptable and perfect." — **Romans 12:2**

Boys are in trouble. More than ever, they're being intentionally misled and confused by an anti-Christian culture that wants to destroy their faith in Jesus Christ.

Secular worldviews—including relativism and humanism—also want to devour your son's heart and mind, and thereby control his thoughts and actions.

To withstand these attacks, boys need to be well-grounded in God's Word. Romans 12:2 instructs us not to give in to worldly philosophies. Instead, we are to transform our minds and lives by imitating the characteristics of Christ.

To withstand the enemy's attacks, you've got to fight lies with truth. And the greatest of all weapons is the sword of the Spirit, which is the Word of God.

CLIMB HIGHER

How important is the Bible in your home? Does it sit on a shelf from Sunday to Sunday, or do you open its pages and allow it to transform you?

How can you encourage your son to study the Bible for himself? What techniques or resources might help him better understand the importance of God's guidance in our day-to-day lives?

‹ **LOUISIANA** › Located just south of Hammond, Louisiana, the **Joyce Wildlife Management Area** features a 0.5-mile out-and-back trail into the beautiful cypress swamplands. The trail features several overlooks from which to observe the bountiful wildlife. 🚶🚶

Detours

73

"I will instruct you and teach you in the way you should go." — **Psalm 32:8a**

As you drive down the highway, you encounter many road signs. But one of the most annoying signs is the detour. When our plans of traveling to a destination are hindered, we grow frustrated by the delay and inconvenience.

Detours, however, don't only happen on the highway. The parenting journey also has them. Perhaps you love football, but your son doesn't. Maybe he likes to read, but you'd rather wrestle with him in the living room. He may have a passion for algebra, but numbers make your head spin.

Whatever the detour to your parenting plans and expectations, take comfort in knowing that God is in control. That detour you find so annoying may be the very thing God uses to accomplish His will in the future.

Of course, detours test our patience. That's why it's vital to steer your thoughts toward the mind of Christ. By trusting God even when you cannot see where life's road is taking you, you'll have confidence that He will continue guiding you throughout the twists and turns of life.

CLIMB HIGHER

As you travel through parenthood, are you allowing the Lord to steer your life?

If you have expectations for your son that aren't coming true, are you crashing into frustration or wisely navigating toward a new destination?

‹ NEW JERSEY ›

Paterson Great Falls National Historical Park is a small urban outdoor area in Patterson, New Jersey, northwest of New York City. The park features a 1.5-mile hiking trail with views of imposing waterfalls.

Facing Fear

"Be strong and courageous. Do not be frightened, and do not be dismayed, for the Lord your God is with you wherever you go." — **Joshua 1:9**

Fear and anxiety are attacking kids across the country. That's a fact.

According to the Center for Disease Control, over 7% of children have been diagnosed with anxiety. That's around 4.5 million kids!

There are many reasons for this anxiety, worry about finding friends at school, and even dread about what the future holds. Then, of course, there's nervousness about finances, social turmoil, and even world conflicts.

As a parent, remind your son that even when the world feels out of control, we can have confidence that God reigns supreme.

God's Word emphasizes that God is in control, with many verses about overcoming fear and being courageous. Deuteronomy 31:6 tells us that He will never leave us or forsake us. What a wonderful promise!

CLIMB HIGHER

What fears does your son face? Do you think they're ridiculous, or do you acknowledge them before helping your son work through them?

Romans 12:2 talks about the "renewing of your mind." What does that mean? How can it help your son put fear in proper context?

Take time to read Psalm 27:1, Isaiah 41:10, and John 14:27.

‹ **WASHINGTON** › The Marymere Falls Trail, not far from Joyce, Washington, is an excellent way to immerse yourself in the awe-inspiring beauty of one of the Pacific Northwest's greatest gems—**Olympic National Park**. This 1.7-mile round-trip hike weaves through evergreen scenery and climaxes with dazzling views of Lake Crescent. 🥾🥾

Wonderfully Created

75

"For the Lord sees not as man sees: man looks on the outward appearance, but the Lord looks on the heart."— **1 Samuel 16:7b**

Did you know that 30% of teen boys use unhealthy techniques to control their weight? Skipping meals, vomiting. Even taking laxatives!

Parents with boys in this category wish there were 3 simple steps to help their sons escape the downward spiral of self-image and self-esteem problems. But it's not that easy.

In addition to consulting doctors for help, here's something else you should do. Remind your son that we are His workmanship—wonderfully created in His image.

To help emphasize this, show your son Bible verses like Psalm 100:3, Ephesians 2:10, and Revelation 4:11. He'll see God as the perfect Creator who is caring and compassionate.

As you invest time and attention in your son, he will also realize how much you really love him.

CLIMB HIGHER

If your son struggles with self-image problems, what might be the root cause of this? How does his environment or friends contribute to his mental health?

It's easy for boys to think they are too fat, or short, or just plain common. Talk to your son about struggles you faced as a kid and how you overcame those obstacles. A real-life story goes a long way in illustrating a solution.

‹ **VERMONT** › The 2-mile Mount Philo Western Loop is located in **Mount Philo State Park** near Charlotte, Vermont. It is a moderately challenging route with incredible views of the nearby Adirondacks Mountains across the river in New York. Though the New England winters are long and snowy, this trail remains in use all year long, especially for snowshoeing and cross-country skiing. 🏃🏃

Time Is Ticking

76

"Look carefully then how you walk, not as unwise but as wise, making the best use of the time, because the days are evil."
— **Ephesians 5:15-16**

Each day contains 1,440 minutes. That may seem like a bunch of time, but it passes by in a flash. The same can be said for weeks, months, and even years.

Time is passing quickly . . . that's a fact. But here's another fact: You don't want to look back on your parenting years with regret. Don't allow the busyness of work, hobbies, and other activities to pull you away from investing time and attention in your son. Because—before you know it—your son will be grown up and heading out into the world.

Ephesians chapter 5 reminds us to redeem the time because the days are evil. But how do we do this? Begin by making sure your priorities are properly focused. How much time do you spend watching TV versus spending time with your son?

Be intentional about having one-on-one time with your son. You'll never regret the memories you make together.

CLIMB **HIGHER**	The routines of life have a way of pushing family aside. What can you do to prioritize family time?
	Even a few minutes can make a big difference in connecting with your son. What's something you and your son could do together—today?

‹ **Kansas** › Located in the **Konza Prairie Natural Area** near Manhattan, Kansas, the Konza Prairie Loop is a 2.7-mile hike showcasing the prairie terrain of America's heartland. Don't miss the Hokanson Homestead, connected to the trail by a short spur. This homestead, built in 1878, evokes a bygone age of pioneers carving out a life for themselves in these fertile plains. 🚶🚶

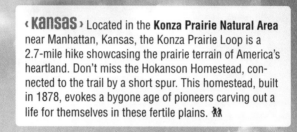

The Greatest Adventure

77

"I will not set before my eyes anything that is worthless. I hate the work of those who fall away; it shall not cling to me."
— Psalm 101:3

Boys love stories, especially action-packed tales of danger and excitement.

But beware. Too often, the content they read online or in books and magazines is crude, sensual, and violent. Even worse, many of the books written specifically for boys carry unbiblical worldviews. Secular authors are strategically influencing boys in unhealthy ways, confusing them about what's right or wrong, moral or immoral.

That's why it's important that you help your son find action and adventure in the pages of a book that builds up his character. Encourage him to dive into fascinating stories about missionaries and evangelists. Additionally, many explorers, inventors, and scientists have great testimonies of faith. Their stories of reliance on God are just as exciting as fiction.

By inspiring your son through godly role models, you show him that the greatest adventure in life is found in following God.

CLIMB HIGHER

Do you know what your son is reading in books and magazines? What kind of content is he reading or watching online?

Research age-appropriate books that encourage your son to follow the Lord. Consider reading the same book he's reading. Then take time to discuss it together.

‹ **FLORIDA** › The **Black Bear Wilderness Area Trail**, located 20 miles north of Orlando, Florida, is a 7-mile loop through some of Florida's most picturesque wetlands. The raised boardwalk trail offers hikers the chance to wander through the swampy area while staying (mostly) dry. The wetlands are teeming with life in many forms, so keep your eyes peeled and bring plenty of bug spray. 🚶🚶

Why?

"For as the heavens are higher than the earth, so are my ways higher than your ways and my thoughts than your thoughts." — **Isaiah 55:9**

78

Do unanswered *why* questions frustrate you? Perhaps there's that nagging question about *why* your son has to suffer with a physical deformity or chronic health condition. Or it could be that your son isn't as athletic, intellectual, or social as you'd like.

When you feel hot under the collar because of unanswered questions, don't give up hope. And don't doubt God's goodness.

In Isaiah 55, God reminds us that we don't understand everything, but He does. And because the God of the universe has you and your son's best interests in mind, He will provide peace even when *why* questions puzzle, pester, and perplex you.

As a dad, you wish you could understand the reason life is sometimes hard, painful, and unfair. Your responsibility, however, is to exercise faith in God's plan and purpose. You can depend on Him.

CLIMB

HIGHER

Is there an unanswered *why* question causing bitterness to poison your heart? What's the antidote to feelings of resentment?

When your son begins asking his own *why* questions, how can your words and advice build up his Christian faith?

167

‹ **CALIFORNIA** › At only 0.4 miles, the trek to **McWay Falls** overlook is a short, easy hike near Big Sur, California. But don't write this hike off due to its modest length. It offers a picturesque view of the falls and the ocean beyond, perfect for a quiet outdoors lunch or watching the sun set over the Pacific. Keep your eyes peeled for whales and California condors. 🚶🚶

Music to Your Ears

*"Oh come, let us sing to the Lord;
let us make a joyful noise to the rock
of our salvation!"* — **Psalm 95:1**

79

Ludwig van Beethoven is recognized by many as one of the greatest composers of all time. But did you know that he wrote five sonatas and his famous Ninth Symphony while completely deaf? The secret to his success was his passion for music. That and a whole bunch of hard work and dedication.

As parents, we may not have the musical genius of Beethoven, but we can still create wonderful harmony within our homes. Begin by providing your son a consistent tempo of training, and a steady melody of encouragement. Add to that an upbeat rhythm of physical fun and the vibrato of adventure.

The resulting chords of growth will prepare your son to perform his own creative solo. And in doing this, his life will be a lasting crescendo that brings glory to the Conductor of his life.

CLIMB HIGHER

Is your son's behavior on key, or do his actions fall flat?

When you hear that your son is doing right even when you're not around, that's definitely music to the ears. Do you stand and cheer when his life vibrates the melody of God's love?

‹ **WEST VIRGINIA** › Long Point Trail in **New River Gorge National Park** near Fayetteville, West Virginia, is a captivating 3-mile hike that showcases the splendor of the dramatic New River Gorge. The bridge, completed in 1977, is the third tallest bridge in the US, towering 876 feet above the river. 🥾

I'm Sorry

80

"Therefore, confess your sins to one another and pray for one another, that you may be healed. The prayer of a righteous person has great power as it is working."
— **James 5:16**

Two of the most difficult words for a parent to say are, "I'm sorry." Are you saying them enough?

As a dad, there may be times when you lose your temper, don't control your tongue, or jump to conclusions without gathering the necessary facts. When this happens, do you ask for forgiveness from your son?

The difficulty is that it's easy to feel vulnerable, inadequate, and even humiliated when apologizing.

But here's the truth: Your son will grow to love and respect you even more if you apologize. Humbling yourself demonstrates a love so strong that you're willing to admit wrong in order to restore the relationship.

Saying sorry is tough, but your example goes a long way in helping your son see what true spiritual maturity looks like.

CLIMB HIGHER

When was the last time you apologized to your son? Or if you've never done that, are you saying you've never made a parenting mistake?

What are the elements of a genuine apology? How can your apology be an important moment in helping your son grow emotionally and spiritually?

‹ **NEW MEXICO** › The South Piedra Lisa Trail—located in the **Sandia Mountain Wilderness** near Albuquerque, New Mexico—is a 4.3-mile hike, memorable for peaceful meadows, hardy forests, and breathtaking views. Of note is the nearby Sandia Peak Tramway, the longest passenger tram ride in the world which carries guests to the crest of the mountain at an elevation over 10,000 feet. 🚶🚶

Prayer and Protection

81

"Do not be anxious about anything, but in everything by prayer and supplication with thanksgiving let your requests be made known to God." — **Philippians 4:6**

More than one million American homes are burglarized every year. That's why home video cameras are more popular than ever.

But wouldn't it be great if you could as easily monitor your son's activities when he's away from home? That way you could make sure he isn't being harassed by school bullies or tempted to do wrong when hanging out with his buddies.

Even though you can't monitor your son 24/7, you can do something more effective. You can pray!

- Pray that God guards his heart and mind as he scrolls through social media.
- Pray that God provides him friends that encourage him to do right.
- Pray that God helps him stand for truth even when it isn't easy.

Of course, guiding your son in practical ways is also essential, but never forget the powerful potency of prayer.

CLIMB HIGHER

Because there's a spiritual war going on for your son's heart and mind, he needs your prayers. How regularly do you pray for him?

Are your prayers generic, or do they specifically target your son's needs? When a prayer is answered, do you thank the Lord?

‹ **Indiana** › The Turkey Run Outer Loop, located within **Turkey Run State Park** near Marshall, Indiana, is a 6.3-mile hike showcasing the ravines and waterfalls which make this state park perfect for outdoor adventures. The hike is considered moderately challenging, though hikers can easily extend or abbreviate their trek using the park's network of interconnected trails. 🚶🚶

Scars

"There is one whose rash words are like sword thrusts, but the tongue of the wise brings healing." — **Proverbs 12:18**

82

Can you point to a scar on your body? Perhaps, as a kid, you cut your arm when falling off your bike, or scraped a leg while climbing a tree.

Some boys think scars are cool because they tell an exciting story. But not all scars are visible.

Emotional scars often hurt more than physical wounds. When correcting your son, what kind of vocabulary are you using? During moments of intense frustration and anger, hateful speech can scar a boy's personality. It can also puncture his enthusiasm and bruise his love and trust. Even a parent's tone of voice and facial expressions can cause deep wounds that may not easily heal.

When correcting your son, ask the Holy Spirit to guide your thoughts and actions. When you're emotionally under control, you'll provide instruction that leads to growth, instead of resentment. By intentionally relying on God when you feel emotionally activated, you'll leave your son with valuable lessons instead of invisible scars.

CLIMB HIGHER

Based on your son's age and personality, what methods do you use to correct his bad behavior?

When it's necessary to provide discipline, are you in control of your words, emotions, and actions?

‹ **MISSISSIPPI** › The **Vicksburg Military Park** North Loop, near Vicksburg, Mississippi, provides hikers with a chance to get outside and immerse themselves in American history. The 3.5-mile route meanders over gently rolling hills and solemn groves overlooking the battleground. Along the trail, you'll see numerous memorials, Civil War Era cannons, and plaques with information about the men who fought and died on these grounds. 🚶🚶

Coffee

"Oh, taste and see that the Lord is good! Blessed is the man who takes refuge in him!" — **Psalm 34:8**

83

It's Saturday morning. You had hoped to get some extra sleep, but your kids are already running around the house. There's a roar of activity down the hallway.

As you drag yourself out of bed and pour yourself a cup of coffee, take a moment to consider this COFFEE acrostic:

C stands for *Christ*. Draw closer to him!

O stands for *opportunity*. Parenting is a privilege, even when it tests your patience.

F stands for *faith*. Keep Christ first in all that you do.

F also stands for *family*. Stick by each other through thick and thin.

E stands for *eternity*. Teach your kiddos to set their affections on things above.

E also stands for *energy*. Trust God to provide you strength to keep on keeping on.

Now take a sip. Isn't that good? Now that you've got your coffee, it's time to investigate what that crash in the living room was all about!

CLIMB HIGHER

There are dozens of ways to brew coffee. There are even more ways to train a son. How would you describe your parenting technique?

Are you relying on God for strength? Are you searching His Word for guidance?

‹ RHODE ISLAND › The **Arcadia State Management Area** near West Greenwich, Rhode Island, is a peaceful forest haven. Within that management area, the Ben Utter Trail, a 2.7-mile hike along Wood River, is perfect for a quiet afternoon in God's creation.

A Spark

"And let us consider how to stir up one another to love and good works . . . encouraging one another, and all the more as you see the Day drawing near."
— **Hebrews 10:24-25**

84

Ever strike a match?

A single match—or even a single spark from flint and steel—can start a fire. And if provided with enough fuel, that spark can quickly grow into a large and powerful force.

The same can be said for words. A simple word of encouragement could be the spark that encourages your son to accomplish incredible things.

If your son is struggling with school or sports or social activities, give him some tips and pointers in a patient way. But never overlook the power of verbal encouragement. Tell your son that you believe in him and that you know he can accomplish whatever he puts his mind to. Then, when you see progress, give him a high five and say, "Awesome job!"

This simple act of encouragement could spark your son to keep on trying his best. It's amazing how small words of support can lead to big results.

CLIMB HIGHER

Today's culture tells guys not to depend on other people. But Ecclesiastes 4:9-10 says that two are better than one because they can help and encourage one another. When was the last time you complimented your son? How did he react?

‹ **MISSOURI** › Located 26 miles from Branson, Missouri, the **Dogwood Canyon Nature Park** features a flat trail surrounded by serene groves. The well-maintained trail is 6.2 miles there and back, with ample opportunities to spot rainbow trout as you walk along the creek. You'll come across several waterfalls and ponds, so factor in some time to pause and appreciate the sights and sounds along the way. 🏃🏃

Squeaky and Rusty

"Rather, speaking the truth in love, we are to grow up in every way into him who is the head, into Christ." — **Ephesians 4:15**

85

When a door hinge squeaks or a bike chain becomes rusty, what do you spray on it? Probably WD-40. The spray lubricant works so well that around 80% of American households have a can somewhere in their garage.

But WD-40 wasn't easy to create. Engineers developed dozens of mixtures until formula number 40 proved just right.

The next time you see a can of WD-40, remember that good things take time to develop. It's easy to become annoyed when your son doesn't mature as quickly as you'd like. Maybe he squeaks out excuses or is rusty at basic life skills. Maybe his words are coated in grime, or his actions clank and clatter against your household rules.

Even though mental, emotional, and spiritual growth takes time, God is faithful. He'll never give up on your son, and neither should you. Do your part in consistently training your son, and then, after that, leave the results in God's capable care.

CLIMB
___

HIGHER

Even if parts of your son's life are squeaky and rusty, are you committed to helping him grow? How do you handle frustration?

What role does positive encouragement have in helping him move forward more smoothly?

‹ **ALABama** › Just east of Fort Payne, Alabama, **Little River Canyon National Preserve** is a stunning natural wonderland with abundant wildlife, wooded canyons, and scenic waterfalls. The Little River Canyon trail is a 1.4-mile hike with moderate elevation gain.

The Wheels on the Bus

"A joyful heart is good medicine, but a crushed spirit dries up the bones."
— **Proverbs 17:22**

86

Y ou know that irritating song, "The wheels on the bus go round and round"? Well, the routines of parenthood sometimes feel as if they just keep rolling along, round and round, day after day.

Wake up—get the kids ready for school—make breakfast—clean up messes—drive to work—finish work—drive home—help the kids with homework— and so on and so forth.

When the routines of life feel repetitive, intro- duce new ways to keep boredom at bay. In the car, play Bible trivia together. At the dinner table, tell funny stories about your childhood. Before bedtime, listen to an audiobook.

Even though life continues day after day, find ways to trans- form tedious tasks into amusing adventures. Not only will this make life more fun for your kiddos, but for you as well.

CLIMB HIGHER

God created life to be fully enjoyed. Are you setting an example of what a joyful life looks like?

Your home doesn't have to be an amusement park to be fun. Some of the best fun happens when you and your family share laughs. In what specific ways are you helping to create an atmosphere of fun and trust at home?

‹ FLORIDA › **Lettuce Lake Park Hammock Trail** near Tampa, Florida, is a 1.2-mile loop offering fast access to a captivating sample of wetlands wildlife. Even though the trail is paved and well maintained, the park still feels remote and wild. Before you head out the door, make sure to grab your binoculars and keep an eye out for birds, snakes, rabbits, and alligators. 🚶🚶

Poison

"Create in me a clean heart, O God, and renew a right spirit within me."
— Psalm 51:10

87

What poisonous plant is easily identified by its "leaves of three"?

If you said poison ivy, you're right! When you see its "leaves of three," you immediately step back. That's because nobody wants red, itchy skin covered in bumps and blisters.

In the great outdoors, it's important to teach your son the hazards of poison ivy, but it's even more important to teach him the hazards of lust and sensuality. Today's secular culture sexualizes women in movies and magazines. They're objectified on the internet and throughout social media.

For guys who want to guard their thoughts and do what's right, it's a tough world out there.

Fortunately, your son isn't alone. If he's trusted Christ as his Savior, the Holy Spirit provides strength and discernment. Remind him of Philippians 4:8. Point out those things that are true, pure, and virtuous. In doing so, you'll guide him away from the hazardous poisons that cause terrible pain.

CLIMB HIGHER

Have you talked to your son about how to resist temptation? How would you recommend he guard his thoughts?

What Bible verse could you memorize together that talks about the importance of purity?

‹Kansas› **Mushroom Rock State Park**, near Brookville, Kansas, is known for its unique rock formations. At only 0.2 miles, the Mushroom Rock Trail leads hikers from the parking lot to a cluster of rocks that bear an uncanny resemblance to mushrooms. 🥾🥾

Work and Inspiration

"But you, take courage! Do not let your hands be weak, for your work shall be rewarded." — **2 Chronicles 15:7**

I n 1962, the Soviet Union was winning the Space Race. To inspire the nation, President Kennedy announced, "We choose to go to the Moon." He admitted that this wouldn't be easy, but that America would prevail.

Through an incredible program built on sweat, setbacks, and successes, NASA launched astronauts to the moon in July 1969. As Neil Armstrong took the first step on the lunar surface, Americans stared at television screens in awe and inspiration.

Indeed, achievement is built on the backbone of hard work. But it's competition that spurs us to even greater heights of progress. That's why it's unfortunate that today's society of increasing entitlement tells parents that competition harms a boy's self-esteem when he loses.

Even though losing isn't fun, it's by trudging through loss that we can then enjoy the thrill of victory. By inspiring your son to conquer obstacles, he'll develop the knowledge, skills, and fortitude to succeed in life.

CLIMB HIGHER

Are you inspiring your son to try hard things? When he experiences failure and setbacks, do you encourage him to continue onward?

Everyone needs encouragement. Do you praise your son's successes, including small triumphs and major victories?

‹ **PENNSYLVANIA** › **Cherry Springs State Park**, near Coudersport, Pennsylvania, is a popular destination for stargazers. Its interpretive trail, the only trail located within the park, is a 1-mile hike featuring educational displays on the importance of forests and forestry. While many who visit the park come for the after-dark views of the celestial lights, the interpretive trail is also a great way to explore the forest during the daytime. 🚶🚶

Provide a Helping Hand

89

"Open your mouth for the mute, for the rights of all who are destitute. Open your mouth, judge righteously, defend the rights of the poor and needy."
— **Proverbs 31:8-9**

When your son was young, did he ever point at someone in a wheelchair? Do your older kids whisper about the new kid who stutters or has a deformity?

Teach your kids never to make fun of someone with a handicap. Because we live in a sin-cursed world where physical and mental challenges exist, these handicaps make life hard for people with these disabilities.

We may not be able to make handicaps go away but, as Christians, we can show courtesy, compassion, and the love of Christ. Teach your son to hold the door open for someone in a wheelchair. Teach your kids to listen patiently to someone who stutters. Demonstrate how to show patience with someone who doesn't understand how to behave normally in public.

By helping your kids treat people kindly, they'll focus less on the handicap and more on the person's personality.

CLIMB HIGHER

Kids often tease one another, but that doesn't mean it's right. How can you teach your son to stick up for those who are being bullied or mistreated?

Not all handicaps are visible. Mental illness can be just as difficult and exhausting as a physical deformity. Is your son struggling emotionally? What might be some signs that he needs help?

‹ KENTUCKY › **Cumberland Falls State Park**, near Parkers Lake, Kentucky, features wooded mountains and dramatic waterfalls, making this an excellent hiking destination. Eagle Falls Trail, a 1.8-mile hike, traverses rugged terrain to the 69-foot Cumberland Falls.

Up a Creek ...

"Fear not, for I have redeemed you; I have called you by name, you are mine. When you pass through the waters, I will be with you; and through the rivers, they shall not overwhelm you." — **Isaiah 43:1-2**

90

Boys love adventure. That's why paddling a canoe across a lake or along a river is a time-tested way to exercise their minds and bodies.

But have you ever heard the phrase, "Up a creek without a paddle"? It refers to being in a dangerous situation where you can't get yourself out of the problem or predicament.

As your son grows up, don't let him be stranded "up a creek without a paddle." Trials and challenges will try to sink his faith. Turbulent waters will try to knock his emotional health off course. But by teaching your son how to manage stress, learn life skills, and seek God's guidance, you'll prepare him to navigate choppy waters to reach the shore of success.

CLIMB HIGHER

A paddle is an essential tool in operating a canoe. It enables the user to pull himself and his canoe forward through the water. What paddles (tools and resources) does your son use in steering through the stormy seas of life?

As your son continues through youth and adolescence, how can you show him the way around dangerous obstacles?

‹ **NORTH DAKOTA** › **White Butte**, the highest point in North Dakota, rises out of the surrounding grassland just outside of Amidon, North Dakota. The trailhead is off Highway 85 between mile markers 43 and 44. The 3.4-mile roundtrip trail provides a great opportunity to check out the expansive views from atop White Butte. 🚶🚶

Only One Life

"Yet you do not know what tomorrow will bring. What is your life? For you are a mist that appears for a little time and then vanishes." — **James 4:14**

What's your favorite sport? Is it basketball? Maybe it's football? What about track or tennis?

For C. T. Studd, his passion was cricket—a baseball-like game played in England. As a professional cricket player, Studd shocked the sports world when he announced his decision to become a missionary to China.

He later said, "Only one life, 'twill soon be past, Only what's done for Christ will last."

What about you? Are you using your life in meaningful ways? How can you do that in the town or city where God has placed you?

As a parent, one of your most important responsibilities is investing time and attention in your son. As you guide him in studying the Bible and loving the Lord Jesus, you honor the Lord with your words and actions.

Life passes faster than we ever expect. Make today count. Train your son in the way he should go.

CLIMB HIGHER

When you're old and gray, how do you want to remember your past? What memories will you treasure?

What life changes can you make now that will help you better prepare your son for the future?

‹ **Delaware** › The Walking Dunes Trail is a 2.6-mile loop through Delaware's **Cape Henlopen State Park**. Located near the mouth of the Delaware Bay, the park features peaceful forests and striking coastal sand dunes. For views of the Atlantic, there are multiple easy beach access points branching off the loop. 🏃🏃

Hands-On Learning

"What you have learned and received and heard and seen in me—practice these things, and the God of peace will be with you." — **Philippians 4:9**

92

When Benjamin Franklin's name is mentioned, kids usually think of the guy who placed a metal key on a kite string. Talk about a "shocking" experience!

Many adults, however, recognize Benjamin Franklin as one of America's most important Founding Fathers. In addition to helping write the Declaration of Independence, he also had great advice about the learning process. He said, "Tell me and I forget. Teach me and I remember. Involve me and I learn."

Because kids each have their own mind and personality, they learn in many different ways. A girl may be able to sit still, hear instruction, and understand completely. A boy, however, often benefits from physical participation.

It's one thing to tell your son how to do something but having him actually do it through hands-on involvement helps him remember and apply the lesson in a much more effective way.

The key to discovering how your son learns best is by spending time with him. Are you doing that?

CLIMB HIGHER

In what ways does your son learn best? Are you using physical exercise and outdoor activities to help him grow physically, mentally, and spiritually?

‹ **NORTH CAROLINA** › Affording commanding views of the surrounding **Blue Ridge Mountains**, the Blackrock Mountain Trail near Waynesville, North Carolina, is a 4.8-mile trek through some of the most striking scenery in the Carolinas. Just off of the Blue Ridge Parkway, the trailhead is easily accessible, though the trail itself is somewhat challenging. 🚶🚶

Beautiful Feet

"I pray that the sharing of your faith may become effective for the full knowledge of every good thing that is in us for the sake of Christ." — **Philemon 1:6**

93

Did you know that your feet contain around a quarter of all the bones in your body? It's true! Each foot contains 26 bones, 33 joints, and over 100 ligaments, tendons, and muscles.

From a medical standpoint, feet are amazing. But Romans 10:15 gives a different perspective. The verse says, "How beautiful are the feet of those who preach the good news."

Sharing the good news of salvation is incredibly important. But this doesn't come naturally. That's why your son needs you to show him the way.

When you leave a tip at a restaurant, include a gospel tract. When an unsaved relative stops by for supper, pray for your food as you normally would. When you're in line at the hardware store, start up a conversation with another dad about the greatest gift you've ever received—the gift of eternal life.

Then, if your son has accepted Christ as his Savior, encourage him to share his own testimony. The more you and your son proclaim the gospel to others, the more you honor Christ through your lives.

CLIMB HIGHER

What evangelistic activities could you and your son do together?

How does your perspective of eternity affect how you see people?

‹ **Minnesota** › **Chester Park**, in Duluth, Minnesota, has a beautiful 2.4-mile loop with a walking bridge over a waterfall tumbling down into a jagged rocky ravine. While tucked away in the heart of the city, this hike offers a scenic escape into God's creation. 🚶🚶

Knots

*"That their hearts may be encouraged,
being knit together in love."*
— Colossians 2:2

94

When building an outdoor shelter, rope comes in handy. But do you know how to tie a square knot? What about a sheet bend knot or a bowline knot?

It takes time and practice to master these knots, but when you understand their purpose and how to tie them, life becomes a little easier and a whole lot more fun.

The same is true in parenting. Raising boys can feel like a rope full of knots. There's twisting and turning as your son matures, and crossing and coiling as he transitions into adolescence. During this time, patience is essential. If you rush the formation process, you'll experience chaos and confusion. That's enough to get your stomach tied up in knots.

When your son's emotions loop out of control, spend extra time with him. Your presence and guidance will help him sort through the tangle of fears, temptations, and uncertainties he faces in today's world. And as you point him to Christ, those knots in the parenting process will transform into useful tools that help your son stay secure in his faith.

CLIMB HIGHER

Remember, you're "knot" alone. Parenting may feel like a tangled mess, but there are many excellent programs and resources to help you along the journey. What tools are you using to stay knit together with your son?

‹ **OHIO** › Ohio's **Cuyahoga Valley National Park**, a 33,000-acre natural haven between Cleveland and Akron, is a perfect place for a day-hike. Plateau Trail, a 4.6-mile loop, guides hikers through the beautiful park, past quiet ponds and aromatic pine forests. 🚶🚶

Chameleon

"Let love be genuine. Abhor what is evil; hold fast to what is good." — **Romans 12:9**

95

What comes to mind when someone mentions a chameleon?

Most people think of the scaly lizard that changes color based on its surroundings. They can even adapt the brightness of their skin for strategic purposes.

Chameleons are fascinating, but they're NOT an example of how Christians should act in today's world. Believers should demonstrate genuine behavior in word *and* action.

As a dad, realize that your son is watching you. Is your speech consistent regardless of whether you're at work or on the sports field? Are your values at church consistent with how you act while on vacation?

Don't be a chameleon. Instead, through consistency of character, show your son how to honor the Lord in each and every area of life.

CLIMB HIGHER

You want to set a good example for your son, but that isn't always easy. If he hears you tell an inappropriate joke or catches you staring at something you've told him is wrong, what do you do? Do you hope he'll forget your words and actions or do you admit your mistakes?

How can you use your own faith journey to help him grow spiritually?

‹ NEW HAMPSHIRE › Tucked away in the woods west of the White Mountains, New Hampshire's **Franconia Notch State Park** is a hiker's paradise with majestic mountains, deep blue lakes, and tranquil forests. The Lonesome Lake Trail is a 3-mile hike which shows off a worthy sampling of the park's attractions. 🚶🚶

Dealing with Death

"My flesh and my heart may fail, but God is the strength of my heart and my portion forever." — **Psalm 73:26**

96

Has your son experienced the death of a pet? What about the loss of a friend or of a grandparent?

Death is a hard concept for young kids to understand. But even for children who are older, emotions can quickly spiral out of control. And without a proper perspective of what this loss means, death's grip can drag kids into anger, despair, and loneliness.

When death steals a loved one away, take time to answer your son's questions. Remind him that even Jesus cried when his friend Lazarus died. Grief is natural, but we have a God who promises to provide comfort. Psalm 34:18 says, "The Lord is near to the brokenhearted and saves the crushed in spirit."

Although loss is inevitable, use grief as an opportunity to help your son rely on God for strength. Point him to the hope of our salvation.

CLIMB HIGHER

Are you there for your son during the highs and lows of life? If his hermit crab dies, how do you respond?

How can loss and death motivate us to use our time wisely? What legacy do you want to leave your son even after the Lord calls you home?

‹ **Indiana** › When you think of Indiana, you probably don't picture sandy beaches and tall, winding dunes next to deep blue waters. Yet, that is precisely what you'll find at **Indiana Dunes National Park**. Trail 9, a 3.8-mile loop leads hikers through the sandy terrain. From atop the hills and dunes, you'll see Lake Michigan to one side and a flat, forested land-scape stretching to the horizon on the other side. 🚶‍♂️🚶‍♀️

Bow-wow!

"Greater love has no one than this, that someone lay down his life for his friends."
— John 15:13

97

Nearly 70% of Americans own a pet. But can you guess what kind of pet is the most popular?

If you answered *dog*, you're right! From pugs to poodles and beagles to bulldogs—canine companions share a place in our house and in our hearts.

Dogs are definitely cute, but they're also a great way to connect with kids. When it's time for your son to walk Duffy or Max, head out the door with them.

As you walk together, talk to your son. This doesn't mean asking, "How was your day?" and waiting for him to answer, "Fine." Ask questions that invite him to share the excitement and frustrations he's experiencing, like:

- What's something funny that happened at school today?
- What part of [sports or hobby] do you like the best? What about the worst?
- When was the last time you wanted to give up? What made you feel that way?

Spend more time listening to your son. He'll see that you're actually his best friend.

CLIMB HIGHER

It's easy to ask questions just to gather day-to-day information, but are you also asking your son questions that dig deeper into his emotional and spiritual life?

‹ **MASSACHUSETTS** › **Great Brook Farm State Park** in Carlisle, Massachusetts, is a great place to enjoy the charming New England countryside to the northwest of the Boston metro area. The Woodchuck, Chicken, and Beaver Loop is a 5.2-mile hike through thick woods and serene ponds, perfect for fishing or a picnic lunch. 🥾

Lemons

98

"Not only that, but we rejoice in our sufferings, knowing that suffering produces endurance, and endurance produces character, and character produces hope." — **Romans 5:3-4**

Have you ever seen a boy bite into a lemon? If so, his face probably scrunched up into wrinkles because of the super sour taste.

We all experience sour moments. Maybe your son loves basketball. But then, while making a simple layup before the big game, he sprains his ankle and has to sit the bench. Or perhaps for the science fair, he builds the Eiffel Tower out of spaghetti noodles. But in the middle of the night, it's clawed apart by your cat.

During times of unexpected frustration, remind your son that God is in control. And because God loves him with an unconditional love, the heartaches and headaches of life won't seem quite so bad.

When you help your son stir in the sweet realization that he can depend on God for strength, the Lord will transform life's lemons into lesson-learning lemonade.

CLIMB HIGHER

What a boy struggles with at age 6 is different from what he struggles with at age 16. What challenges is your son currently facing? How can you provide advice and encouragement? How can you do this in both word and action?

‹ **CONNECTICUT** › The Wadsworth Falls Loop, near Middlefield, Connecticut, is a 3.6-mile hike through **Wadsworth Falls State Park**. The trail guides hikers along Laurel Grove Brook with views of the falls toward the middle of the loop. 🚶‍♂️🚶

Terrific Texts

"Let no corrupting talk come out of your mouths, but only such as is good for building up, as fits the occasion, that it may give grace to those who hear."
— **Ephesians 4:29**

99

Do you use your phone to send text messages? According to statistics, around 80% of Americans do. Those text messages are often sent to family, friends, and co-workers. And now, more than ever, millions of children also carry a smartphone.

If you've decided to provide your son a phone, make sure he uses it responsibly. But in addition to that, use text messaging as a way to connect with him. If you're out of town during one of his sporting events, send a quick text:

> Hey, Buddy. You're in my thoughts and prayers. Just wanted you to know I'm rooting for you.

Or if you hear that he placed 2nd in an academic bowl or music competition, text:

> Whoo-hoo! Way to go. I'm super proud of you!

A text message doesn't take long to type, but the encouragement it provides lasts for days.

CLIMB HIGHER

Does your son have a phone or tablet? If so, how can you use technology to strengthen his character and family relationships?

209

‹ **IDAHO** › Located in **Sawtooth National Forest**, the Proctor Mountain Trail is a 4.2-mile loop near Sun Valley, Idaho. The Sawtooth forest showcases views of four separate mountain ranges, though you'll have to come ready to earn those views as you'll gain 1,076 feet of elevation along the trail. 🏃🏃

First Aid

"Beloved, I pray that all may go well with you and that you may be in good health, as it goes well with your soul."
— 3 John 1:2

When out in the woods, accidents happen. A boy may sprain his ankle, scratch his legs, or burn a finger. When accidents happen, a first aid kit comes in handy. The medical supplies within the kit help alleviate pain and provide healing.

As a dad, don't you wish that parenting boys came with its own first aid kit? If it did, it'd definitely include an ice pack to cool high tempers, bandages for wrapping hurt feelings, and ointment to sooth away frustration.

Optional accessories might include aspirin for headache relief during those teenage years, antiseptic wipes to disinfect against worldly influences, and an emergency blanket for needed rest.

Even though you may not have a parenting first aid kit, you can still provide your son consistent comfort and care. A little time and attention goes a long way in helping him heal from the bruising effects of today's secular society.

CLIMB HIGHER

We spend a lot of time and money ensuring our sons have proper physical care. But are you also making sure your son has proper emotional and spiritual health?

What antibiotic can help him heal when infected by worldly influences?

‹ **ARIZONA** › Providing stunning views of the **Grand Canyon** in Arizona, the Rim Trail stretches for 12.1 miles—though shuttles make it possible to pick shorter segments of the trail to hike. Overlooks along the trail will take your breath away as you praise God for His spectacular creation. This is one of the most rewarding hikes in the region and is an excellent location from which to view sunrise or sunset. 🏃

Legacy

"A good name is to be chosen rather than great riches, and favor is better than silver or gold." — **Proverbs 22:1**

101

No one wants to think about death, but if you're a Christian, you know that Christ has conquered the grave. Still, at some point, physical death will separate you from your family. The question is: What kind of legacy will you leave behind. How will your son remember you?

Billy Graham, one of the most widely known evangelists of the 20th century, said, "The greatest legacy one can pass on to one's children and grandchildren is a legacy of character and faith."

There's nothing wrong in being remembered for your work accomplishments or athletic abilities. It's fine for people to remember your custom motorcycle, barbecue-grilling skills, and hearty laugh. But, in the end, your son will most appreciate the time and attention you invested in his life.

The days, weeks, and months pass faster than we ever imagine. Are you building a legacy of character and faith?

CLIMB HIGHER

What things are most important to you in life? How do you spend your hours when not at work?

When the flashy enticements of the world try to distract you, how do you stay focused on your God-given role of being a dad?

Index of Trails by State

The author is grateful to the following Unsplash photographers

Additional Photo Credits

Raw data for our trail descriptions are drawn from AllTrails.com. All trail descriptions are our own.

Could Your Greatest Victory Be One Courageous Answer Away?

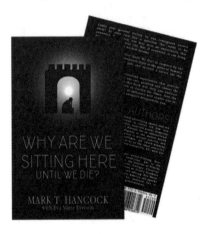

In *Why Are We Sitting Here Until We Die*, visionary author and CEO, Mark T. Hancock, draws inspiration from the biblical account of the desperate leper at the gates of Samaria. Within these pages, Hancock unearths precious wisdom from the text, skillfully guiding readers to:

- discern the times,
- discover the cause,
- harness the power,
- leave the gate,
- embrace the challenge,
- and ultimately live out the unique calling that God has placed on their lives.

Are you ready to embark on a transformative journey toward your greatest triumph?

Order here

Ready for S'more Real World Adventure?

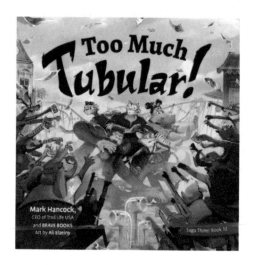

Too many boys are lost in digital worlds of phones, televisions, and video games. In this captivating children's book from BRAVE Books and Trail Life USA, Team BRAVE embarks on a rescue mission to save the animals of Furenzy Park, who have lost themselves in a virtual reality. Sharing s'mores around a roaring campfire, the BRAVE Books heroes learn important lessons about moderation, sharing, outdoor adventure, spending time as a family, and face-to-face connection.

Order here

Free Resources for

Boys have big questions that routinely go unanswered: "What does it mean to be a man?" "Where do I belong?" "What are my boundaries, and why are they set?" "Why should I even try?"

In a culture lacking any clear vision of positive masculinity,

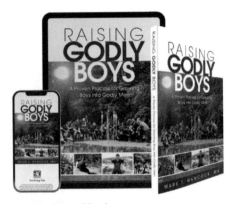

we must provide boys with a template. This short book provides answers and lays out a Proven Process to Guide, Ground, Appreciate, and Inspire boys in a manner that reverses the rising tide of cultural confusion and preserves a legacy for the men engaged in making a difference.

Order this FREE E-book here

The Trail Life USA Proven Process for Growing Boys into Godly Men

Boys are often unguided, ungrounded, unappreciated, and uninsipred. Trail Life USA seeks to change that.

Raising Godly Boys

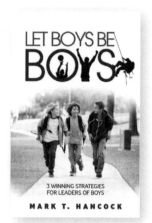

Boys and Girls are different. "As leaders of boys in schools, homeschools, churches, and youth organizations, we must recognize and affirm their unique strengths and challenges. We are positioned to instill the principles and character traits that can prepare boys to become courageous, successful, focused men. But will we?"

How can we successfully engage and disciple boys? If your attempts look anything like a typical classroom or Sunday school class, you are fighting a losing battle. Boys aren't defective, they are different and to engage and disciple them effectively, we must Let Boys be Boys!

Order this FREE
E-book here

Discover three winning strategies from counselor and author Mark T. Hancock to engage and guide the next generation of young men to honor God, lead with integrity, and serve others.

One Minute. One Broadcast. Every Day

The Raising Godly Boys Minute is a daily 60-second broadcast designed to help you learn to raise boys to become godly men.

Trail Life USA is where boys thrive! Established on time-less values derived from the Bible and set in the context of outdoor adventure, over 60,000 Trailmen are engaged in a Troop setting with male mentors where they are challenged to grow in character, understand their purpose, serve their community, and develop practical leadership skills to carry out the mission for which they were created.

Join the Adventure!

Find a Troop near you or start one today.

Learn more at www.TrailLifeUSA.com

Trail Life

Adventure › Character › Leadership